Contents

Instant Pot Vegetable Broth

prep: 5 mins cook: 55 mins additional: 50 mins total: 1 hr 50 mins
Servings: 12
Ingredients

- 3 eaches carrots, unpeeled, halved
- 1 large onion, halved
- 2 stalks celery, halved
- 2 cloves garlic, halved
- 1 teaspoon whole black peppercorns
- 1 teaspoon salt
- 4 sprigs fresh thyme
- 1 sprig fresh rosemary
- 12 cups water

Directions
Step 1
Combine carrots, onion, celery, garlic, peppercorns, salt, thyme, rosemary in a multi-functional pressure cooker (such as Instant Pot). Cover with water. Close and lock the lid. Select high pressure according to manufacturer's instructions; set timer for 30 minutes. Allow 25 minutes for pressure to build.
Step 2
Release pressure using the natural-release method according to manufacturer's instructions, about 30 minutes. Unlock and remove the lid.
Step 3
Let broth sit for 20 minutes to cool. Pour liquid through a strainer and discard all solids.
Nutrition Facts
Per Serving:
14.8 calories; protein 0.4g 1% DV; carbohydrates 3.4g 1% DV; fat 0.1g; cholesterolmg; sodium 219.3mg 9% DV.

Instant Pot Beef and Veg Stew

prep: 15 mins cook: 1 hr 10 mins additional: 5 mins total: 1 hr 30 mins
Servings: 4

Ingredients

- 1 pound extra lean stewing beef, cut into bite-sized pieces
- 2 tablespoons olive oil, or more to taste
- 1 large onion, diced
- 3 cloves garlic, finely chopped
- 1 splash red wine
- 3 cups chopped carrots
- 2 cups chopped celery
- 1 ½ cups canned diced tomatoes
- 1 ½ cups chicken broth
- 1 sprig chopped fresh thyme
- 1 bay leaf
- 1 pinch salt and ground black pepper to taste
- ⅓ cup chicken broth
- 2 tablespoons cornstarch

Directions
Step 1
Heat oil in the pot of an electric pressure cooker set on Saute mode. Add beef; cook until browned on all sides, about 5 minutes. Add onion and cook, stirring constantly, until soft, 3 to 5 minutes. Add garlic; cook until fragrant, about 1 minute.
Step 2
Pour wine into the pot and bring to a boil while scraping the browned bits of food off the bottom with a wooden spoon to deglaze. Add carrots, celery, and tomatoes; stir well. Add 1 1/2 cups chicken broth, thyme, bay leaf, salt, and pepper.
Step 3
Close and lock the lid. Select Meat/Stew option or high pressure according to manufacturer's instructions; set timer for 35 minutes. Allow 10 to 15 minutes for pressure to build.
Step 4
Mix 1/3 cup broth with cornstarch to make the slurry.
Step 5
Release pressure carefully using the quick-release method according to manufacturer's instructions, about 5 minutes. Unlock and remove the lid. Select Saute option and bring mixture to a boil. Slowly add in the slurry. Let simmer until stew thickens slightly, 3 to 5 minutes.
Cook's Note:
Use any extra-lean cut of beef you like.
Nutrition Facts
Per Serving:
464.8 calories; protein 24.3g 49% DV; carbohydrates 24.4g 8% DV; fat 29.4g 45% DV; cholesterol 78.8mg 26% DV; sodium 975.8mg 39% DV.

Instant Pot Keto Crustless Spinach and Gouda Quiche

prep: 10 mins cook: 35 mins additional: 10 mins total: 55 mins
Servings: 4
Ingredients

- 1 tablespoon butter
- 6 eaches eggs
- ½ cup heavy cream
- ½ teaspoon sea salt
- ¼ teaspoon ground black pepper
- ¼ teaspoon ground nutmeg
- 3 cups chopped spinach
- 1 onion, chopped
- 1 cup shredded Gouda cheese
- 1 ½ cups water

Directions
Step 1
Grease a 1 1/2-quart souffle dish with butter.
Step 2
Whisk eggs, cream, salt, pepper, and nutmeg in a bowl. Stir in spinach, onion, and Gouda cheese. Pour into the prepared souffle dish.
Step 3

Turn on a multi-functional pressure cooker (such as Instant Pot). Place water in the pot and add the trivet. Place the prepared dish on the trivet with an aluminum sling, folding ends on top. Close and lock the lid. Select high pressure according to manufacturer's instructions; set timer for 25 minutes. Allow 10 to 15 minutes for pressure to build.

Step 4

Release pressure using the fast-release method, about 5 minutes. Open and remove the lid. Lift quiche by grabbing the ends of the foil sling. Let cool for 5 minutes.

Nutrition Facts

Per Serving:

251.7 calories; protein 15.1g 30% DV; carbohydrates 11.6g 4% DV; fat 17.4g 27% DV; cholesterol 281.7mg 94% DV; sodium 496.1mg 20% DV.

Instant Pot Chicken Soup

prep: 30 mins cook: 38 mins additional: 10 mins total: 1 hr 18 mins

Servings: 8

Ingredients

- 1 tablespoon olive oil
- 5 stalks celery, diced
- 1 large onion, diced
- 2 small heads garlic, peeled and chopped
- 1 (32 fluid ounce) container chicken bone broth
- 1 (32 fluid ounce) container chicken broth
- 4 eaches boneless chicken thighs, cut into 1-inch pieces
- 2 eaches boneless skinless chicken breasts, cut into 1-inch pieces
- 1 (8 ounce) package baby carrots
- 2 tablespoons herbes de Provence
- 1 tablespoon chicken broth base (such as Superior Touch™ Better Than Bouillon™)
- 1 ½ teaspoons red pepper flakes
- 1 pinch salt and ground black pepper to taste
- 2 eaches bay leaves

Directions

Step 1

Turn on a multi-functional pressure cooker (such as Instant Pot) and select Saute function. Add oil, celery, onion, and garlic. Saute until slightly softened, 3 to 5 minutes.

Step 2

Mix bone broth, chicken broth, chicken thighs, chicken breasts, carrots, herbes de Provence, broth base, red pepper flakes, salt, pepper, and bay leaves into the pot. Close and lock the lid. Select low pressure. Set timer for 25 minutes. Allow 10 to 15 minutes for pressure to build.

Step 3

Release pressure using the natural-release method according to manufacturer's instructions, 10 to 40 minutes. Remove bay leaves before serving.

Nutrition Facts

Per Serving:

176.3 calories; protein 17.7g 35% DV; carbohydrates 9.4g 3% DV; fat 7.4g 11% DV; cholesterol 54.6mg 18% DV; sodium 1190.3mg 48% DV.

Grandma's Porcupine Meatballs in the Instant Pot

prep: 15 mins cook: 20 mins additional: 10 mins total: 45 mins
Servings: 4
Ingredients

- 1 pound ground beef
- ½ cup uncooked white rice
- 1 small onion, finely chopped
- 1 egg
- 1 teaspoon diced garlic
- 1 pinch salt and ground black pepper to taste
- 2 (10.75 ounce) cans condensed tomato soup
- ½ cup water

Directions
Step 1
Mix beef, rice, onion, egg, garlic, salt, and pepper in a bowl until combined. Divide mixture into 8 equal portions and form into meatballs.
Step 2
Place meatballs in a multi-functional pressure cooker (such as Instant Pot). Mix tomato soup and water and pour over meatballs.
Step 3
Close and lock the lid. Select high pressure according to manufacturer's instructions; set timer for 10 minutes. Allow 10 to 15 minutes for pressure to build.
Step 4
Release pressure using the natural-release method according to manufacturer's instructions, 10 to 40 minutes.
Nutrition Facts
Per Serving:
438.6 calories; protein 24g 48% DV; carbohydrates 40.6g 13% DV; fat 20.1g 31% DV; cholesterol 114.6mg 38% DV; sodium 950.9mg 38% DV.

Instant Pot Chicken with Barbecue Sauce

prep: 5 mins cook: 10 mins additional: 15 mins total: 30 mins
Servings: 2
Ingredients

- 4 cups water
- 1 (1 ounce) package dry ranch dressing mix (such as Hidden Valley Ranch)
- 1 tablespoon poultry seasoning
- 1 tablespoon ground black pepper, or to taste
- 4 teaspoons salt
- 2 large frozen skinless, boneless chicken breast halves
- 1 (18 ounce) bottle barbeque sauce

Directions
Step 1

Whisk water, ranch dressing mix, poultry seasoning, pepper, and salt together in the bottom of a multi-functional pressure cooker (such as Instant Pot). Add chicken breasts. Close and lock the lid. Select high pressure according to manufacturer's instructions; set timer for 3 minutes. Allow 7 to 10 minutes for pressure to build.

Step 2
Release pressure using the natural-release method according to manufacturer's instructions, 13 to 18 minutes. Unlock and remove the lid. Shred chicken with 2 forks. Coat with barbecue sauce.

Editor's Note:
Nutrition data for this recipe includes the full amount of seasoning mixture. The actual amount of seasoning consumed will vary.

Nutrition Facts
Per Serving:
677.6 calories; protein 47.7g 95% DV; carbohydrates 101.6g 33% DV; fat 6.4g 10% DV; cholesterol 129.2mg 43% DV; sodium 8579.4mg 343% DV.

Instant Pot Pilau Rice

prep: 10 mins cook: 20 mins additional: 10 mins total: 40 mins
Servings: 6
Ingredients

- 1 tablespoon vegetable oil
- ½ teaspoon cumin seeds
- ¼ cup diced red onion
- ¾ tablespoon garam masala
- ½ teaspoon ground turmeric
- ½ teaspoon salt
- 1 ½ cups vegetable broth
- 1 cup uncooked basmati rice, rinsed and drained
- ½ cup frozen peas and carrots
- 1 bay leaf

Directions
Step 1
Turn on a multi-functional pressure cooker (such as Instant Pot) and select Saute function. Heat oil in the pot. Add cumin seeds and stir until they just start to pop. Stir in onion and cook until they begin to soften, about 2 minutes. Season with garam masala, turmeric, and salt. Add vegetable broth, rice, frozen peas and carrots, and bay leaf; stir until well combined.

Step 2
Close and lock the lid. Select high pressure according to manufacturer's instructions; set timer for 5 minutes. Allow 10 to 15 minutes for pressure to build.

Step 3
Release pressure using the natural-release method according to manufacturer's instructions, 10 to 40 minutes. Manually release any remaining pressure. Unlock and remove the lid. Remove bay leaf. Taste rice and adjust seasoning if necessary before serving.

Nutrition Facts
Per Serving:
151.2 calories; protein 3.2g 6% DV; carbohydrates 28.5g 9% DV; fat 3.1g 5% DV; cholesterolmg; sodium 321.3mg 13% DV.

Instant Pot Applesauce

prep: 15 mins cook: 15 mins additional: 15 mins total: 45 mins
Servings: 30
Ingredients

- 1 lemon
- 1 cinnamon stick
- 1 (1/4 inch thick) slice fresh ginger
- 1 star anise pod
- 2 eaches whole cloves
- 1 piece cheesecloth
- 3 pounds apples - peeled, cored, and quartered
- ½ cup water
- ½ teaspoon salt
- 2 tablespoons brown sugar, or more to taste

Directions
Step 1
Use a vegetable peeler to remove 2 thick strips of lemon peel, being careful to avoid the bitter pith. Tie up lemon peel, cinnamon stick, ginger, star anise, and cloves in cheesecloth for easy retrieval after cooking.
Step 2
Place apples in a multi-functional pressure cooker (such as Instant Pot). Add cheesecloth bundle, water, and salt. Close and lock the lid. Select high pressure according to manufacturer's instructions; set timer for 5 minutes. Allow 10 to 15 minutes for pressure to build.
Step 3
Release pressure using the natural-release method according to manufacturer's instructions, 15 to 20 minutes. Avoid releasing pressure manually as hot applesauce may splutter up through the vent. Remove the cheesecloth bundle with a slotted spoon and discard.
Step 4
Mix brown sugar into the applesauce until dissolved. Taste and adjust the level of sweetness if needed.
Cook's Notes:
I planned to use this applesauce in cakes so I didn't want it to be too sweet. Adjust the levels of sweetness and acidity (with lemon juice) to your taste.
Applesauce freezes well. Just be sure to allow enough headroom as you fill the jar or container, as it will expand when frozen.

Nutrition Facts
Per Serving:
28.4 calories; protein 0.2g; carbohydrates 7.7g 3% DV; fat 0.1g; cholesterolmg; sodium 39.9mg 2% DV.

Instant Pot Sausage Queso

prep: 10 mins cook: 25 mins additional: 5 mins total: 40 mins
Servings: 8
Ingredients

- 1 pound bulk country sausage
- 1 tablespoon olive oil
- 1 small onion, chopped
- 1 large jalapeno pepper, seeded and diced
- 1 teaspoon chili powder
- ½ teaspoon ground cumin
- 1 (12 fluid ounce) can or bottle light beer
- 1 (10 ounce) can diced tomatoes with green chiles
- 2 cups shredded sharp Cheddar cheese
- 2 cups shredded Monterey Jack cheese

Directions
Step 1
Crumble sausage in a large skillet and cook over medium-high heat until no longer pink, about 5 minutes. Drain excess grease.
Step 2
Turn on a multi-functional pressure cooker (such as Instant Pot) and select Saute function. Add olive oil, onion, and jalapeno; cook for 3 minutes. Add chili powder and cumin and cook for 2 minutes more. Stir in sausage, beer, and tomatoes. Close and lock the lid. Select Manual; set timer for 5 minutes. Allow 10 to 15 minutes for pressure to build.
Step 3
Release pressure using the natural-release method according to manufacturer's instructions, about 5 minutes. Carefully release remain pressure manually. Remove the lid. Add Cheddar and Monterey Jack cheeses; whisk vigorously until melted. Serve immediately.
Cook's Note:
If you are not serving immediately, you can use the Keep Warm setting, but you will need to stir every 20 minutes to keep the cheese from clumping.
Nutrition Facts
Per Serving:
412.9 calories; protein 28.4g 57% DV; carbohydrates 3.8g 1% DV; fat 31.1g 48% DV; cholesterol 107.3mg 36% DV; sodium 893.6mg 36% DV.

Instant Pot Classic Hummus

prep: 10 mins cook: 45 mins additional: 5 mins total: 1 hr
Servings: 8
Ingredients

- 1 cup dry garbanzo beans
- 3 cups vegetable broth
- ⅓ cup lemon juice
- 3 tablespoons tahini
- 2 tablespoons olive oil
- 2 cloves garlic, chopped
- 1 teaspoon ground cumin
- ½ teaspoon salt

Directions
Step 1
Combine garbanzo beans with vegetable broth in a multi-functional pressure cooker (such as Instant Pot). Close and lock the lid. Select high pressure according to manufacturer's instructions; set timer for 35 minutes. Allow 10 to 15 minutes for pressure to build.
Step 2
Release pressure carefully using the quick-release method according to manufacturer's instructions, about 5 minutes. Unlock and remove lid.
Step 3
Strain garbanzo beans, saving 2/3 cup liquid. Place garbanzo beans in the bowl of a food processor; add lemon juice, tahini, olive oil, and garlic. Blend until smooth and creamy, about 3 minutes. Scrape bowl and add reserved 2/3 cup liquid, cumin, and salt; blend for 1 minute more.
Nutrition Facts
Per Serving:
170.2 calories; protein 6.3g 13% DV; carbohydrates 19.5g 6% DV; fat 8.2g 13% DV; cholesterolmg; sodium 331mg 13% DV.

Instant Pot Haluski

prep: 15 mins cook: 35 mins additional: 15 mins total: 1 hr 5 mins
Servings: 10
Ingredients

- 5 cups water
- 1 (12 ounce) package medium egg noodles
- 1 tablespoon salt
- 1 pound bacon, cut into 1-inch cubes
- ½ cup butter
- 1 teaspoon minced garlic
- 1 head cabbage, diced
- 1 onion, diced
- 1 pinch seasoning blend (such as Morton Nature's Seasons Seasoning Blend), or to taste

Directions
Step 1
Combine water, noodles, and salt in a multi-functional pressure cooker (such as Instant Pot). Push noodles down with a spoon. Close and lock the lid. Select high pressure according to manufacturer's instructions; set timer for 1 minute. Allow 10 to 15 minutes for pressure to build.
Step 2
Release pressure using the natural-release method according to manufacturer's instructions for 6 minutes. Unlock and remove the lid. Set noodles aside.
Step 3
Set the Instant Pot to Saute function. Saute bacon on Medium until browned and crisp, 5 to 7 minutes. Do not drain grease. Add butter and stir until melted. Stir in garlic. Stir in cabbage and onion. Close and lock the lid.
Step 4
Select high pressure according to manufacturer's instructions; set timer for 5 minutes. Allow 10 to 15 minutes for pressure to build.

Step 5
Release pressure carefully using the quick-release method according to manufacturer's instructions, about 5 minutes. Unlock and remove the lid. Mix in egg noodles and seasoning blend.
Cook's Note:
Use whatever seasoning you prefer to taste.
Nutrition Facts
Per Serving:
325.3 calories; protein 12g 24% DV; carbohydrates 32.1g 10% DV; fat 17.1g 26% DV; cholesterol 69mg 23% DV; sodium 1171.2mg 47% DV.

Creamy Keto Chicken-Poblano Soup

prep: 10 mins cook: 30 mins additional: 10 mins total: 50 mins
Servings: 4
Ingredients

- 4 eaches skinless, boneless chicken thighs
- 1 pinch salt and ground black pepper to taste
- 10 ounces water
- 1 (10 ounce) can diced tomatoes with green chile peppers
- 1 poblano pepper, sliced
- ½ onion, diced
- 8 ounces cream cheese, softened

Directions
Step 1
Season chicken thighs liberally with salt and black pepper.
Step 2
Combine water, tomatoes, poblano pepper, and onion in a multi-functional pressure cooker (such as Instant Pot). Add chicken. Close and lock the lid. Choose Meat setting and set the timer for 17 minutes. Allow 10 to 15 minutes for pressure to build.
Step 3
Release pressure using the natural-release method according to manufacturer's instructions for 5 minutes. Release remaining pressure carefully using the quick-release method according to manufacturer's instructions, about 5 minutes. Unlock and remove the lid.
Step 4
Remove chicken from the pot and shred. Add cream cheese to the soup in the pot and stir until mixed well. Return shredded chicken to the pot and mix well.
Nutrition Facts
Per Serving:
396.5 calories; protein 23g 46% DV; carbohydrates 6.5g 2% DV; fat 31.2g 48% DV; cholesterol 126.4mg 42% DV; sodium 546.9mg 22% DV.

Instant Pot Low Country Boil

prep: 15 mins cook: 35 mins additional: 5 mins total: 55 mins
Servings: 4
Ingredients

- 1 (12 ounce) package andouille sausage, sliced
- 1 ½ pounds baby red potatoes, halved
- 1 medium onion, chopped
- 4 teaspoons seafood seasoning (such as Old Bay)
- 1 (12 fluid ounce) can or bottle beer
- 3 ears corn, husked and cut into thirds
- 12 ounces frozen shell-on shrimp

Directions
Step 1
Combine andouille sausage, potatoes, and onion in a multi-functional pressure cooker (such as Instant Pot). Sprinkle seafood seasoning over the top. Pour in beer. Lay corn pieces on top. Close and lock the lid. Select high pressure according to manufacturer's instructions; set timer for 1 minute. Allow 20 minutes for pressure to build.
Step 2
Release pressure carefully using the quick-release method according to manufacturer's instructions, about 2 minutes. Unlock and remove the lid. Stir in shrimp. Close and lock the lid.
Step 3
Select high pressure according to manufacturer's instructions; set timer for 0 minutes. Allow 10 minutes for pressure to build.
Step 4
Release pressure carefully using the quick-release method according to manufacturer's instructions, about 2 minutes. Unlock and remove the lid.
Cook's Note:
Make sure you use frozen shrimp to prevent overcooking.
Nutrition Facts
Per Serving:
564.7 calories; protein 30.1g 60% DV; carbohydrates 48.3g 16% DV; fat 26g 40% DV; cholesterol 176.4mg 59% DV; sodium 1481.8mg 59% DV.

Red Beans with Rice

prep: 10 mins cook: 1 hr 21 mins additional: 5 mins total: 1 hr 36 mins
Servings: 6
Ingredients

- 3 cups water
- 1 cup dried red beans, rinsed
- 1 tablespoon extra-virgin olive oil, or as needed
- 3 cloves garlic, minced
- 2 ½ cups brown rice

- ½ (1.41 ounce) package sazon seasoning (such as Goya), or to
- taste
- 1 pinch salt to taste

Directions
Step 1
Place water and red beans in a pressure cooker. Close cooker securely and place pressure regulator over vent according to manufacturer's instructions. Adjust heat until regulator is gently rocking. Cook at high pressure for 30 minutes. Let pressure release naturally according to manufacturer's instructions, 5 to 10 minutes; unlock and remove lid.
Step 2
Heat oil in a saucepan over medium heat. Cook and stir garlic until browned, 2 to 3 minutes. Add the water and beans from the pressure cooker. Stir in sazon seasoning and salt. Reduce heat to low; cook until flavors combine, about 3 minutes. Add rice. Cover and simmer until rice is tender and liquid has been absorbed, 45 to 50 minutes.
Nutrition Facts
Per Serving:
214.8 calories; protein 9.4g 19% DV; carbohydrates 37.6g 12% DV; fat 3.2g 5% DV; cholesterolmg; sodium 541.1mg 22% DV.

Instant Pot Chicken and Mushrooms with Gravy

prep: 10 mins cook: 25 mins additional: 25 mins total: 1 hr
Servings: 3
Ingredients

- 6 tablespoons unsalted butter, divided
- 1 tablespoon extra-virgin olive oil
- 1 onion, diced
- 1 pinch salt
- 3 large boneless, skinless chicken breasts, trimmed of fat
- ¼ cup chicken stock, or more to taste
- 1 (16 ounce) package baby bella mushrooms, halved
- 1 tablespoon ranch seasoning mix
- 1 teaspoon steak sauce, or more to taste
- 1 teaspoon Worcestershire sauce, or more to taste
- 1 pinch freshly ground black pepper
- 2 tablespoons all-purpose flour

Directions
Step 1
Turn on a multi-functional pressure cooker (such as Instant Pot) and select Saute function. Add 2 tablespoons butter and olive oil. Add onion and salt; stir occasionally until onion starts to brown.
Step 2
Meanwhile, grease a skillet with 1 tablespoon butter and heat over high heat. Add chicken breasts and cook until browned, about 3 minutes per side.
Step 3

Switch pressure cooker to Warm function. Pour in chicken stock and stir the pot to release any bits stuck on the bottom. Add mushrooms, ranch seasoning, steak sauce, Worcestershire sauce, and pepper. Stir until combined. Place chicken breasts on top, with a small pat of butter on each chicken breast.
Step 4
Close and lock the lid. Select high pressure according to manufacturer's instructions; set timer for 6 minutes. Allow 10 to 15 minutes for pressure to build.
Step 5
Release pressure using the natural-release method according to manufacturer's instructions, about 25 minutes. Transfer chicken breasts and mushrooms to a serving dish. Select Saute function to boil liquid in the pot.

Step 6
Heat remaining 2 tablespoons butter in a saucepan over low heat. Stir in flour until a smooth, thick paste forms, 2 to 3 minutes. Whisk into the liquid in the pot and cook until thickened, 2 to 3 minutes. Adjust seasoning as desired and pour chicken and mushrooms.
Cook's Note:
Deglaze onions with a splash of beer, if preferred.
Nutrition Facts
Per Serving:
550.7 calories; protein 50g 100% DV; carbohydrates 14.5g 5% DV; fat 32.8g 51% DV; cholesterol 178.2mg 59% DV; sodium 424.3mg 17% DV.

Instant Pot Corn Chowder

prep: 10 mins cook: 35 mins additional: 15 mins total: 1 hr
Servings: 8
Ingredients

- 2 tablespoons butter
- 1 onion, diced
- 4 cloves garlic, minced
- 4 cups fresh corn kernels
- 4 cups peeled and diced potatoes
- 4 cups vegetable broth
- ½ teaspoon fresh thyme leaves
- ½ teaspoon paprika
- 1 teaspoon salt
- 1 teaspoon ground black pepper
- 1 cup heavy cream

Directions
Step 1
Turn on a multi-functional pressure cooker (such as Instant Pot) and select Saute function. Add butter and melt. Stir in onion and garlic; cook until onion is soft and translucent, about 5 minutes. Turn off Saute function.
Step 2
Add corn, potatoes, vegetable broth, thyme, paprika, salt, and pepper to the pot; stir to combine. Close and lock the lid. Select high pressure according to manufacturer's instructions; set timer for 15 minutes. Allow 10 to 15 minutes for pressure to build.
Step 3
Release pressure using the natural-release method according to manufacturer's instructions, about 15 minutes. Release any remaining pressure carefully using the

quick-release method according to manufacturer's instructions. Unlock and remove the lid. Remove 1 cup of potatoes and corn to a bowl. Mash with a fork and return to the pot.
Step 4
Select Saute function again and pour in heavy cream. Cook until soup has thickened to desired consistency.
Cook's Note:
Frozen corn may be substituted for fresh, if desired.
Nutrition Facts
Per Serving:
277.9 calories; protein 5.5g 11% DV; carbohydrates 33.6g 11% DV; fat 15.2g 23% DV; cholesterol 48.4mg 16% DV; sodium 569.6mg 23% DV.

Instant Pot Dumpling Soup

prep: 10 mins cook: 20 mins additional: 5 mins total: 35 mins
Servings: 6
Ingredients

- 1 teaspoon sesame oil
- 1 teaspoon olive oil
- 1 tablespoon finely chopped ginger
- 1 teaspoon finely chopped garlic
- 10 cups low-sodium chicken broth
- 1 ½ pounds frozen wontons
- 1 teaspoon dried parsley

- ½ teaspoon salt, or more to taste
- ½ teaspoon freshly ground black pepper
- 2 cups thinly sliced bok choy
- 2 tablespoons low-sodium soy sauce (such as Bragg)
- 4 medium (4-1/8" long)s green onions, thinly sliced

Directions
Step 1
Turn on a multi-functional pressure cooker (such as Instant Pot) and select Saute function. Adjust to Low if necessary. Pour in sesame oil and olive oil. Add ginger and garlic to the hot oil; cook until fragrant without browning, about 1 minute. Add chicken broth, wontons, parsley, salt, and pepper. Break apart any wontons that have frozen together. Close and lock the lid.
Step 2
Select Soup function; set timer for 2 minutes. Allow 10 to 15 minutes for pressure to build.
Step 3
Release pressure carefully using the quick-release method according to manufacturer's instructions, about 5 minutes. Unlock and remove the lid. Mix in bok choy and soy sauce and let sit, stirring occasionally, for 3 minutes. Taste and season with additional salt if necessary.
Step 4
Ladle soup into bowls and top with green onions.

Nutrition Facts
Per Serving:

323 calories; protein 23.2g 46% DV; carbohydrates 37.3g 12% DV; fat 8.7g 13% DV; cholesterol 91.5mg 31% DV; sodium 1349.7mg 54% DV.

Instant Pot Mexican Chicken and Rice

prep: 15 mins cook: 25 mins additional: 15 mins total: 55 mins
Servings: 6

Ingredients

- 2 tablespoons olive oil
- 1 small onion, diced
- 1 small green bell pepper, diced
- 2 cloves garlic, minced
- 1 pound skinless, boneless chicken breasts, cubed
- 1 ½ teaspoons ground cumin
- 1 teaspoon cayenne pepper
- ½ teaspoon salt
- 1 ¼ cups long-grain white rice
- 1 (15 ounce) can black beans, rinsed and drained
- 1 (10 ounce) can diced tomatoes and green chiles (such as RO*TEL)
- 1 ½ cups chicken broth
- 1 cup salsa
- ¾ cup frozen corn
- 1 ½ cups grated Cheddar cheese, or more to taste

Directions
Step 1
Turn on a multi-functional pressure cooker (such as Instant Pot) and select Saute function. Pour oil into the pot and add onion, bell pepper, and garlic. Saute for 2 minutes. Add chicken and season with cumin, cayenne, and salt; stir to combine. Continue cooking until onion is clear and chicken is slightly browned, 2 to 3 minutes. Pour in rice and saute, allowing oil and spices to coat grains.
Step 2
Stir black beans, diced tomatoes, chicken broth, salsa, and corn into the pot. Mix well. Cancel Saute function. Close and lock the lid with vent turned to Sealing. Select high pressure according to manufacturer's instructions; set timer for 8 minutes. Allow 10 to 15 minutes for pressure to build.
Step 3
Release pressure using the natural-release method according to manufacturer's instructions, 10 to 40 minutes. Unlock and remove the lid. Cover the top with Cheddar cheese and replace the lid. Let steam melt the cheese before serving, about 3 minutes.
Cook's Note:
You can use any color of bell pepper that you prefer.
Nutrition Facts
Per Serving:
520.3 calories; protein 33.7g 67% DV; carbohydrates 54.3g 18% DV; fat 18.8g 29% DV; cholesterol 80.8mg 27% DV; sodium 1459.1mg 58% DV.

Greek Style Beef Stew

prep: 35 mins cook: 15 mins additional: 20 mins total: 1 hr 10 mins
Servings: 6
Ingredients

- 1 tablespoon olive oil
- 1 pound cubed beef stew meat
- 1 onion, peeled and chopped
- 1 large clove garlic, minced
- ¼ cup red wine
- 2 tablespoons red wine vinegar
- ½ cup fat-free reduced-sodium beef broth
- 1 tablespoon tomato paste
- ½ teaspoon dried rosemary
- ½ teaspoon dried oregano
- 6 eaches whole black peppercorns
- 2 eaches bay leaves
- 1 teaspoon ground cumin
- ⅛ teaspoon ground cinnamon
- 1 pinch ground cloves
- ¼ teaspoon ground black pepper
- 1 ½ teaspoons light brown sugar
- 1 (28 ounce) can whole plum tomatoes, undrained and quartered
- ½ cup water
- 2 eaches potatoes, peeled and cut into 2-inch pieces
- 2 medium (blank)s carrots, peeled and sliced
- ¼ teaspoon salt to taste

Directions
Step 1
Heat olive oil in a 5-quart pressure cooker over medium-high heat. Add half the beef; cook and stir until well browned on all sides. Remove beef with a slotted spoon and set aside. Brown the remaining meat and set aside.
Step 2
Place chopped onion in the pressure cooker; cook and stir for 1 minute. Add the garlic and stir for an additional minute. Pour in the red wine, red wine vinegar, and beef broth; stir in the tomato paste and mix well.
Step 3
Grind or crush rosemary, oregano, and peppercorns in a mortar and pestle or spice grinder. Add crushed spices to the cooker with bay leaves, cumin, cinnamon, cloves, black pepper, and brown sugar.
Step 4
Pour in tomatoes and their juice; rinse the can with 1/2 cup water and add the water to the cooker. Stir in potatoes and carrots. Return the browned meat to the pressure cooker. A 5-quart pot should be about half full and a little soupy; the potato will dissolve a bit and thicken it after cooking. Cover the pot and seal the lid.
Step 5
Bring the pot up to high pressure over high heat. Reduce the heat to low, maintaining full pressure, and cook for 15 minutes. Remove from heat and let the pressure reduce naturally. Taste the stew and add salt, if desired.

Cook's Notes:
We have this every other week during the winter months. Also the cassia cinnamon popular here in the U.S. is way too strong, so be careful. If you use Ceylon cinnamon, use 1/4 teaspoon.

You can use low-sodium chicken broth instead of the beef broth. If you used canned broth or stock with salt, don't add any more salt. It's very good with homemade veggie stock. This is not as good without tomato paste or bay leaves. I'm sure you could sub tofu for the beef and make it completely vegan, but I will leave that to my vegetarian friends. Great the next day. Enjoy!

This can also be made in a slow cooker. Omit the 1/2 cup water. Use a skillet and follow steps 1 and 2. Transfer contents of the skillet to a slow cooker; add the potatoes and carrots. Place the browned meat on top of the vegetables and add the remaining ingredients. Cover and cook on Low for 8 to 10 hours.

Nutrition Facts
Per Serving:
288.6 calories; protein 15.9g 32% DV; carbohydrates 26.8g 9% DV; fat 13g 20% DV; cholesterol 41.7mg 14% DV; sodium 367.3mg 15% DV.

Instant Pot Easy Maple Syrup Applesauce

prep: 10 mins cook: 18 mins additional: 10 mins total: 38 mins
Servings: 4

Ingredients

- 2 ½ pounds apples - peeled, cored, and chopped
- 3 tablespoons water
- 2 tablespoons maple syrup
- 1 cinnamon stick
- ¼ teaspoon nutmeg
- 1 pinch salt

Directions
Step 1
Combine apples, water, maple syrup, cinnamon stick, and nutmeg in a multi-functional pressure cooker (such as Instant Pot). Close and lock the lid. Select high pressure according to manufacturer's instructions; set timer for 8 minutes. Allow 10 to 15 minutes for pressure to build.
Step 2
Release pressure using the natural-release method according to manufacturer's instructions, 10 to 40 minutes. Unlock and remove lid. Remove cinnamon stick and season with salt. Blend with an immersion blender to the desired consistency.

Nutrition Facts
Per Serving:
176.6 calories; protein 0.8g 2% DV; carbohydrates 46.6g 15% DV; fat 0.6g 1% DV; cholesterolmg; sodium 42.9mg 2% DV.

Instant Pot Easy Chicken Marsala

prep: 15 mins cook: 35 mins additional: 15 mins total: 1 hr 5 mins
Servings: 4
Ingredients

- 3 eaches boneless chicken breasts, cut into strips
- 1 ½ teaspoons salt , divided
- ½ teaspoon ground black pepper, divided
- 3 tablespoons butter, divided
- 2 tablespoons olive oil, divided
- 2 cloves garlic, chopped
- 2 tablespoons minced shallots
- 1 cup button mushrooms, sliced
- 1 cup chicken broth
- ⅔ cup Marsala wine
- ¼ cup water
- 1 tablespoon cornstarch
- ½ cup heavy whipping cream
- 1 tablespoon chopped fresh parsley

Directions
Step 1
Season chicken breasts with 1/2 teaspoon salt and 1/4 teaspoon pepper. Turn on a multi-functional pressure cooker (such as Instant Pot) and select Saute function. Heat 1 tablespoon butter and 1 tablespoon olive oil; cook chicken breasts on both sides until golden brown, about 5 minutes. Remove chicken from the pot. Melt remaining 2 tablespoons butter and 1 tablespoon olive oil; add garlic and shallots; cook until softened, about 3 minutes. Stir in mushrooms and cook until tender, about 3 minutes. Pour chicken broth into the pot and bring to a boil while scraping the browned bits of food off the bottom of the pan with a wooden spoon for deglazing, about 3 minutes. Return chicken to the pot and cover with Marsala wine. Close and lock the lid. Select Poultry function; set timer for 10 minutes. Allow 10 to 15 minutes for pressure to build.
Step 2
Release pressure using the natural-release method according to manufacturer's instructions, about 10 minutes. Release remaining pressure using the quick-release method, about 5 minutes. Unlock and remove the lid. Select Saute function. Dissolve cornstarch in water and stir into the pot with heavy whipping cream. Season with remaining teaspoon salt and 1/4 teaspoon pepper; cook until sauce has slightly thickened, about 5 minutes. Serve and sprinkle with fresh parsley.
Nutrition Facts
Per Serving:
414.8 calories; protein 18.6g 37% DV; carbohydrates 10.9g 4% DV; fat 28.4g 44% DV; cholesterol 109.1mg 36% DV; sodium 1278.7mg 51% DV.

Pressure Cooker Paella with Chicken Thighs and Smoked Sausage

prep: 15 mins cook: 40 mins additional: 10 mins total: 1 hr 5 mins
Servings: 6
Ingredients
- 2 tablespoons olive oil
- 4 eaches bone-in, skin-on chicken thighs
- 1 pinch salt to taste
- 6 ounces smoked sausage, diced
- 1 medium sweet onion (such as Vidalia), diced
- 1 red bell pepper, chopped
- 3 cloves garlic, minced
- 1 ½ cups medium-grain white rice
- 1 ½ teaspoons smoked paprika
- 1 ½ teaspoons ground turmeric
- 1 pinch cayenne pepper

- 1 pinch saffron
- ¼ cup dry sherry
- 2 ¾ cups chicken broth
- 1 (10 ounce) can diced tomatoes
- ½ cup frozen peas

Directions
Step 1
Turn on a multi-functional pressure cooker (such as Instant Pot) and select Saute function. Add olive oil and warm for 1 to 2 minutes.
Step 2
Season chicken thighs with salt. Place chicken skin-side down in the oil. Cook until skin is golden, 4 to 6 minutes. Slide a spatula underneath several times to prevent skin from sticking to the pot. Turn and cook until other side is lightly browned, 2 to 3 minutes. Transfer chicken thighs to a plate.
Step 3
Add sausage, onion, and bell pepper to the pot. Saute until onion is softened, about 3 minutes. Stir in garlic and cook until fragrant, about 1 minute. Add rice, paprika, turmeric, cayenne, and saffron. Stir constantly until spices are aromatic and rice becomes translucent and shiny.
Step 4
Pour in sherry and cook until absorbed, about 1 minute. Cover ingredients with chicken broth. Scrape any browned bits off the bottom of the pot. Turn off Saute setting and place chicken thighs on top of the rice. Turn pressure regulator to sealing position; select Manual and set cooking time for 12 minutes at high pressure. Allow 10 to 15 minutes for pressure to build.
Step 5
Release pressure using the natural-release method for 10 minutes according to manufacturer's instructions. Turn pressure regular to 'venting' and release remaining pressure. Remove lid, take out chicken thighs, and pour in tomatoes and peas. Mix well.
Step 6
Switch to Saute mode and cook until liquid is mostly evaporated, 3 to 5 minutes more. Top each serving of rice with a chicken thigh.
Nutrition Facts
Per Serving:
494.1 calories; protein 23.7g 47% DV; carbohydrates 47.2g 15% DV; fat 21.8g 34% DV; cholesterol 64.8mg 22% DV; sodium 1173.8mg 47% DV.

Instant Pot Orange-Cranberry-Balsamic Pork Loin

prep: 15 mins cook: 30 mins additional: 5 mins total: 50 mins
Servings: 6

Ingredients
- 2 pounds pork loin
- 1 pinch salt and pepper to taste
- 2 tablespoons olive oil
- ¼ cup balsamic vinegar
- ½ cup water
- 2 tablespoons all-purpose flour
- 6 ounces cranberries, fresh or frozen

- ½ cup orange juice
- ½ cup water
- ½ cup brown sugar
- ¼ cup orange marmalade
- 1 tablespoon finely minced jalapeno pepper, or to taste
- ½ teaspoon salt
- ¼ teaspoon ground cloves

Directions
Step 1
Season pork loin with salt and pepper. Turn on a multi-functional pressure cooker (such as Instant Pot) and select Saute. Heat olive oil until hot. Add pork loin and brown on each side for a total of about 5 minutes. Remove pork loin and set aside. Add balsamic vinegar to the pot and stir to deglaze, scrapping up all the browned bits.
Step 2
Whisk 1/2 cup water and flour together in a small bowl and add to the Instant Pot, stirring until smooth. Mix in cranberries, orange juice, 1/2 cup water, brown sugar, orange marmalade, jalapeno, 1/2 teaspoon salt, and cloves. Set pork loin on top. Close and lock the lid. Select high pressure according to manufacturer's instructions; Set timer for 12 minutes. Allow 10 to 15 minutes for pressure to build.
Step 3
Release pressure using the natural-release method according to manufacturer's instructions, about 10 minutes. Release remaining pressure carefully using the quick-release method according to manufacturer's instructions, about 5 minutes. Unlock and remove the lid.
Step 4
Remove the pork from the pot, cover with aluminum foil, and let meat rest for 5 minutes. Puree the cranberries using an immersion blender until smooth, or leave them whole if you prefer a chunky sauce.
Cook's Note:
If sauce is too thin, select the Saute button and just cook down for several minutes to thicken. Or you also can thicken by mixing together a small amount of water and cornstarch, and stirring into the sauce.
Nutrition Facts
Per Serving:
402.9 calories; protein 24.9g 50% DV; carbohydrates 36g 12% DV; fat 17.8g 27% DV; cholesterol 73.4mg 25% DV; sodium 289.9mg 12% DV.

Instant Pot Hungarian Goulash

prep: 20 mins cook: 50 mins additional: 15 mins total: 1 hr 25 mins
Servings: 6

Ingredients

- 1 pound beef sirloin, cubed
- ¼ cup all-purpose flour
- 1 tablespoon paprika
- 1 teaspoon cayenne pepper, divided
- ½ teaspoon ground white pepper, divided
- 2 teaspoons olive oil, divided
- 1 teaspoon bacon fat
- 2 cups water

- 2 teaspoons beef base
- 1 onion, chopped
- 1 red bell pepper, chopped
- 2 cloves garlic, chopped
- 1 tablespoon tomato paste
- 2 tablespoons red pepper paste
- ½ teaspoon dried minced shallot
- ¼ cup sour cream

Directions
Step 1
Combine sirloin, flour, paprika, 1/2 teaspoon cayenne, and 1/4 teaspoon white pepper in a bowl. Stir until the meat is completely covered.
Step 2
Heat 1 teaspoon olive oil and bacon fat in a Dutch oven over medium-high heat. Add the meat, shaking off any excess flour; saute until nicely browned on all sides, 5 to 7 minutes. Transfer to a multi-functional pressure cooker (such as Instant Pot). Mix water and beef base together thoroughly in a bowl and pour over the beef.
Step 3
Close and lock the lid. Select high pressure according to manufacturer's instructions; set timer for 20 minutes. Allow 10 to 15 minutes for pressure to build.
Step 4
Meanwhile, heat remaining olive oil in a pan over medium-high heat. Saute onion, bell pepper, and garlic in the hot oil until onion is translucent, 5 to 7 minutes. Add tomato paste and mix together. Reduce heat to low, cover, and set aside.
Step 5
Release Instant Pot pressure using the natural-release method according to manufacturer's instructions for 10 minutes. Release remaining pressure carefully using the quick-release method according to manufacturer's instructions, about 5 minutes. Unlock and remove the lid. Carefully remove the inner pot and use a slotted spoon to transfer the meat to the Dutch oven.
Step 6
Turn the heat up under the Dutch oven to medium and let cook, stirring constantly, about 5 minutes. Add the liquid from the Instant Pot carefully; mix to combine. Add pepper paste, dried shallot, remaining cayenne, and remaining white pepper. Taste for seasoning and cook over low heat until the mixture is thick, about 10 minutes. Garnish with sour cream and serve.
Nutrition Facts
Per Serving:
191.4 calories; protein 14.9g 30% DV; carbohydrates 12.1g 4% DV; fat 9.8g 15% DV; cholesterol 37.7mg 13% DV; sodium 250.2mg 10% DV.

Electric Pressure Cooker Short Ribs

prep: 10 mins cook: 1 hr additional: 15 mins total: 1 hr 25 mins
Servings: 8

Ingredients

- 2 ½ pounds beef short ribs
- 1 tablespoon garlic powder
- 2 teaspoons kosher salt
- 1 ½ teaspoons ground black pepper
- 2 ½ tablespoons olive oil
- 1 cup beef stock
- 1 (6 ounce) can tomato paste
- 2 eaches carrots, coarsely chopped

- 1 onion, coarsely chopped
- ¼ cup balsamic vinegar
- 1 large portobello mushroom cap, chopped
- 2 tablespoons water, or as needed
- 1 tablespoon cornstarch, or as needed
- 1 pinch salt and ground black pepper to taste

Directions
Step 1
Season short ribs on all sides with garlic powder, kosher salt, and pepper.
Step 2
Turn on a multi-functional pressure cooker (such as Instant Pot) and select Saute function according to manufacturer's instructions. Set temperature to 375 degrees F (191 degrees C) if your unit has a temperature setting.
Step 3
Heat olive oil in the pot. Add short ribs; sear all over until golden brown, about 2 minutes per side. Remove from pot and set aside.
Step 4
Combine beef stock, tomato paste, carrots, onion, vinegar, and mushroom in the pot. Stir until tomato paste is dissolved. Return short ribs to the pot. Close and lock the lid. Select Meat function according to manufacturer's instructions; set timer for 30 to 40 minutes. Allow 10 to 15 minutes for pressure to build.
Step 5
Release pressure using the natural-release method according to manufacturer's instructions, about 15 minutes. Unlock and remove the lid. Remove short ribs and skim any fat from the top of the liquid in the pot.
Step 6
Stir water and cornstarch together to make a slurry. Set pressure cooker to Saute and bring the liquid to a boil. Stir in the slurry until mixture is thickened to your liking. Season with salt and pepper and return the short ribs. Cook on low until flavors come together, about 5 minutes more.
Nutrition Facts
Per Serving:
384 calories; protein 15.5g 31% DV; carbohydrates 11.9g 4% DV; fat 30.6g 47% DV; cholesterol 58.3mg 19% DV; sodium 725.4mg 29% DV.

Mensaf (Jordanian Lamb Stew)

prep: 15 mins cook: 55 mins total: 1 hr 10 mins
Servings:
Ingredients

- 4 tablespoons olive oil
- 2 pounds boneless lamb shoulder, cut into 2 inch pieces
- 8 cups water
- 2 cups uncooked white rice
- ¼ cup pine nuts
- 6 eaches pita bread rounds
- 1 cup salted goat's milk (jameed el-kasih)

Directions
Step 1

Place 1 tablespoon olive oil into a pressure cooker over medium-high heat. Add the lamb and cook until evenly browned on all sides. Remove the lamb. Add cooking rack; place lamb on rack. Pour in 4 cups water. Close cover securely; place pressure regulator on vent pipe. Bring cooker to full pressure over high heat. Reduce heat to medium-high; cook for 40 minutes. (Pressure regulator should maintain a slow steady rocking motion; adjust heat if needed.)
Step 2
Remove pressure cooker from heat, and allow pressure to drop on its own. Remove lamb, separate meat from bones, and keep warm. Discard bones. Pour pan broth into a bowl, and set aside.
Step 3
Meanwhile, place remaining four cups water, 1 tablespoon olive oil, and rice into a saucepan; bring to a boil over medium-high heat. Stir, reduce heat, cover, and simmer until all moisture is absorbed, about 20 minutes.
Step 4
Place remaining 2 tablespoons olive oil into a skillet over medium heat. Stir in the pine nuts; cook and stir until deep brown, about 5 minutes.
Step 5
Pour 2 cups of the reserved broth into a large pan. Pour in the goat's milk. Add the lamb to the milk mixture. Simmer over medium heat allowing the lamb to absorb some of the liquid, about 30 minutes.
Step 6
To serve, arrange the pita bread over the bottom of a large platter. Spoon rice over the bread. Place the lamb on top of the rice, and drizzle with any remaining milk mixture. Sprinkle pine nuts over the top.
Nutrition Facts
Per Serving:
544.4 calories; protein 23.4g 47% DV; carbohydrates 59.8g 19% DV; fat 22.6g 35% DV; cholesterol 61.4mg 21% DV; sodium 262.7mg 11% DV.

Slow-Cooked Cashew Chicken

prep: 10 mins cook: 2 hrs 8 mins total: 2 hrs 18 mins
Servings: 6

Ingredients
- ¼ cup cornstarch
- 1 teaspoon ground black pepper
- 2 pounds boneless skinless chicken breast halves, cut into 1-inch pieces
- 1 tablespoon canola oil
- 1 cup roasted unsalted cashews
- ¾ cup reduced-sodium soy sauce
- ⅓ cup rice wine vinegar
- ⅓ cup ketchup
- 3 tablespoons sweet chili sauce
- 2 tablespoons dark brown sugar
- 5 cloves garlic, minced
- 1 tablespoon grated fresh ginger
- ½ teaspoon red pepper flakes
- 2 teaspoons toasted sesame oil
- 4 eaches green onions, sliced diagonally

Directions
Step 1

Combine cornstarch and pepper in a resealable plastic bag. Add chicken pieces and shake bag to coat with cornstarch mixture.
Step 2
Heat oil in skillet over medium-high heat. Brown chicken about 2 minutes on each side. Transfer to a multi-functional pressure cooker (such as Fagor).
Step 3
Combine cashews, soy sauce, rice vinegar, ketchup, sweet chili sauce, brown sugar, garlic, ginger, red pepper flakes, and sesame oil in a bowl. Pour over chicken.
Step 4
Close and lock lid. Select Slow Cook function. Cook on Low until flavors are well combined and chicken is cooked through, about 2 hours. Garnish with green onions.
Cook's Note:
Cashews will be softer if you add them in the beginning of the cooking process. If you like the cashews to have more of a crunch, add them right before serving.
Nutrition Facts
Per Serving:
408 calories; protein 35.2g 70% DV; carbohydrates 28.2g 9% DV; fat 17.8g 27% DV; cholesterol 78mg 26% DV; sodium 1367.5mg 55% DV.

Instant Pot Coconut Cream Chicken Noodle Soup

prep: 20 mins cook: 25 mins total: 45 mins
Servings: 4

Ingredients

- 1 tablespoon canola oil
- 1 yellow onion, chopped
- 2 cloves garlic, chopped
- 4 large carrots, peeled and chopped
- 2 cups chopped spinach
- 2 eaches chicken breasts
- 2 cups elbow macaroni
- 28 fluid ounces chicken stock
- 1 (14 ounce) can coconut cream
- 1 tablespoon sriracha hot sauce
- 1 tablespoon paprika
- 1 pinch salt to taste

Directions
Step 1
Pour oil into the pot and add onion and garlic; turn to the "Saute" setting. Cook, stirring occasionally, until onion is tender, about 10 minutes.
Step 2
Mix carrots and spinach into onion mixture; stir well. Lay chicken on top; add macaroni. Pour chicken stock and coconut cream over macaroni; add sriracha sauce, paprika, and salt.
Step 3
Close lid and cook using the "Manual" setting on high until chicken is no longer pink in the center, about 15 minutes. An instant-read thermometer inserted into the

center should read at least 165 degrees F (74 degrees C). Release pressure through manual release.

Nutrition Facts
Per Serving:
672.7 calories; protein 23.7g 48% DV; carbohydrates 58.5g 19% DV; fat 40.9g 63% DV; cholesterol 29.9mg 10% DV; sodium 892mg 36% DV.

Instant Pot Apple Mango Chutney

prep: 10 mins cook: 30 mins additional: 15 mins total: 55 mins
Servings: 8

Ingredients

- 4 cups mango - peeled, seeded and diced
- 2 cups apples - peeled, cored and chopped
- 1 ¼ cups white sugar
- 1 cup cider vinegar
- 1 (1 inch) piece fresh ginger root, minced
- 1 teaspoon sea salt
- 1 teaspoon paprika
- 1 teaspoon chili flakes
- 1 teaspoon cinnamon
- 4 eaches green cardamom pods
- 4 eaches whole cloves
- ½ teaspoon ground black pepper
- 1 bay leaf

Directions
Step 1
Combine mango, apples, sugar, vinegar, ginger, sea salt, paprika, chili flakes, cinnamon, cardamom, cloves, pepper, and bay leaf in a multi-functional pressure cooker (such as Instant Pot). Close and lock the lid. Select high pressure according to manufacturer's instructions; set timer for 12 minutes. Allow 10 to 15 minutes for pressure to build.
Step 2
Release pressure carefully using the slow-release method according to manufacturer's instructions, about 10 minutes. Release remaining pressure using the quick-release method, about 5 minutes. Unlock and remove the lid. Select Saute function; cook until chutney has thickened, about 10 minutes.
Step 3
Let cool completely before storing in sterilized jars.

Nutrition Facts
Per Serving:
149.9 calories; protein 0.3g 1% DV; carbohydrates 37.2g 12% DV; fat 0.2g; cholesterolmg; sodium 223.8mg 9% DV.

Healthy Instant Pot Orange Chicken

prep: 10 mins cook: 15 mins total: 25 mins
Servings: 2

Ingredients
- ¼ cup vegetable oil
- ¼ cup cornstarch
- ½ teaspoon salt
- ½ teaspoon garlic powder
- ¼ teaspoon Chinese five-spice powder
- 2 (4 ounce) chicken breasts, cut into bite-sized pieces
- Orange Sauce:
- ⅓ cup freshly squeezed orange juice
- ¼ cup water
- 1 tablespoon white vinegar
- 1 tablespoon coconut aminos (soy-free seasoning sauce)
- 1 tablespoon cornstarch
- 1 tablespoon sugar
- 1 teaspoon grated garlic
- 1 teaspoon grated ginger

Directions
Step 1
Turn on a multi-functional pressure cooker (such as Instant Pot) and select Saute function. Add oil.
Step 2
Combine cornstarch, salt, garlic powder, and Chinese five-spice powder in a bowl. Toss chicken in the mixture to coat and shake off excess.
Step 3
Saute coated chicken in the hot oil in the pressure cooker pot until golden brown, about 10 minutes. Remove chicken and allow to drain on a baking sheet lined with paper towels. Clean out the pressure cooker pot.
Step 4
Turn pressure cooker on again and select Saute function. Combine orange juice, water, vinegar, coconut aminos, cornstarch, sugar, garlic, and ginger in the pot and cook, whisking regularly, until thickened, 5 to 10 minutes. Add cooked chicken and toss to coat.
Nutrition Facts
Per Serving:
499.1 calories; protein 24.2g 48% DV; carbohydrates 31.7g 10% DV; fat 30.1g 46% DV; cholesterol 64.6mg 22% DV; sodium 776.3mg 31% DV.

Curry in a Hurry

prep: 5 mins cook: 25 mins additional: 15 mins total: 45 mins
Servings: 4

Ingredients
- 5 cups water
- 1 (14.5 ounce) can diced tomatoes
- 1 (14 ounce) can light coconut milk
- 2 cups red lentils
- 1 cup frozen chopped spinach

- 1 red onion, chopped
- 3 tablespoons tomato paste
- 2 tablespoons curry powder
- 3 cloves garlic, minced
- 2 teaspoons vegetable bouillon base (such as Better Than Bouillon Vegetable Base)
- 1 teaspoon cayenne pepper

Directions
Step 1
Combine water, tomatoes, coconut milk, red lentils, spinach, onion, tomato paste, curry powder, garlic, bouillon base, and cayenne pepper in a multi-functional pressure cooker (such as Instant Pot). Close and lock the lid.
Step 2
Select high pressure according to manufacturer's instructions; set timer for 15 minutes. Allow 10 to 15 minutes for pressure to build.
Step 3
Release pressure using the natural-release method according to manufacturer's instructions, about 10 minutes. Unlock and remove the lid. Stir and let sit for 5 minutes before serving.
Nutrition Facts
Per Serving:
505.2 calories; protein 29.5g 59% DV; carbohydrates 73.1g 24% DV; fat 10.7g 16% DV; cholesterolmg; sodium 587.4mg 24% DV.

Instant Pot Beef Paprika

prep: 15 mins cook: 50 mins additional: 10 mins total: 1 hr 15 mins
Servings: 8

Ingredients
- 2 tablespoons olive oil
- 2 pounds cubed beef stew meat
- 1 pinch salt and ground black pepper to taste
- 2 cloves garlic, minced
- 1 cup diced onion
- Sauce:
- 1 ½ cups water, divided
- ¾ cup ketchup
- 2 tablespoons Worcestershire sauce
- 1 tablespoon brown sugar
- 2 teaspoons salt
- 2 teaspoons smoked paprika
- ½ teaspoon dry mustard
- ⅛ teaspoon cayenne pepper
- 1 dash hot pepper sauce (such as Tabasco)
- 2 tablespoons all-purpose flour

Directions
Step 1
Turn on a 6- or 8-quart multi-functional pressure cooker (such as Instant Pot) and select Saute function. Add olive oil and meat, season with salt and pepper, and saute in batches until browned, 5 to 7 minutes per batch. Remove meat to a plate. Add onion and garlic to the pot and cook until tender and fragrant, about 5 minutes.
Step 2

Return meat to the pot and stir in 1 1/4 cups water, ketchup, Worcestershire sauce, brown sugar, salt, paprika, dry mustard, cayenne pepper, and hot pepper sauce. Cancel Saute function.

Step 3
Close and lock the lid. Select high pressure according to manufacturer's instructions; set timer for 15 minutes. Allow 10 to 15 minutes for pressure to build.

Step 4
Release pressure using the natural-release method according to manufacturer's instructions, about 10 minutes.

Step 5
Blend remaining 1/4 cup water with flour in a small bowl. Gradually stir into the meat mixture and select Saute function. Heat until thickened, about 5 minutes.

Cook's Note:
For the adventurous folks, turn it into stew by adding chopped carrots, green beans, chopped potatoes, and chopped celery.

Nutrition Facts
Per Serving:
297.2 calories; protein 19.5g 39% DV; carbohydrates 12.1g 4% DV; fat 19g 29% DV; cholesterol 62.6mg 21% DV; sodium 941mg 38% DV.

Pressure Cooker Salsa Lime Chicken and Rice

prep: 15 mins cook: 20 mins total: 35 mins
Servings: 4

Ingredients

- 2 eaches frozen skinless, boneless chicken breasts, or more to taste
- ½ cup medium salsa
- ½ cup tomato sauce
- ¼ cup lime juice
- 3 tablespoons olive oil
- 1 teaspoon salt
- ½ teaspoon garlic salt
- ½ teaspoon ground black pepper
- ½ cup shredded Mexican cheese blend, or to taste
- 1 cup uncooked jasmine rice
- 1 cup water, or as needed

Directions
Step 1
Combine chicken breasts, salsa, tomato sauce, lime juice, olive oil, salt, garlic salt, and pepper in an electric pressure cooker.

Step 2
Seal pressure cooker and bring to high pressure according to manufacturer's instructions; cook chicken until no longer pink in the center, 8 minutes for thin frozen breasts and 12 minutes for thick frozen breasts. An instant-read thermometer inserted into the center should read at least 165 degrees F (74 degrees C).

Step 3

Release pressure naturally according to manufacturer's instructions. Open pressure cooker; transfer chicken to a serving dish using tongs. Spoon 1/2 of the cooking liquid over the chicken; top with Mexican cheese.

Step 4

Stir rice into the remaining cooking liquid in the pressure cooker. Add enough water to equal 2 cups of liquid. Seal pressure cooker and bring to high pressure according to manufacturer's instructions; cook for 12 minutes. Let pressure release naturally. Serve rice with chicken.

Cook's Notes:

If you don't like it spicy, just use mild salsa or a can of diced tomatoes.

I only did 2 chicken breasts but you can add 2 more to the same amount of liquid. If using thawed chicken breasts, cook for less time.

If the rice is undercooked, pressure cook for additional time and add more water if needed.

Nutrition Facts

Per Serving:

403.1 calories; protein 19g 38% DV; carbohydrates 44.2g 14% DV; fat 16.8g 26% DV; cholesterol 45.4mg 15% DV; sodium 1318.2mg 53% DV.

Instant Pot Bangers and Mash

prep: 15 mins cook: 35 mins additional: 20 mins total: 1 hr 10 mins
Servings: 3

Ingredients

- 2 pounds potatoes, cut into 1 1/2- inch cubes
- ½ cup water
- 1 pound Irish sausages
- ¼ cup butter
- 2 tablespoons heavy whipping cream, or more to taste
- 1 pinch salt and ground black pepper to taste
- Onion Gravy:
- 2 tablespoons butter
- 1 cup beef broth, divided
- 1 small onion, thinly sliced
- 2 teaspoons all-purpose flour
- ½ teaspoon browning sauce

Directions

Step 1

Combine potatoes and water in a multi-functional pressure cooker (such as Instant Pot). Layer sausages on top of the potatoes. Close and lock the lid. Select high pressure according to manufacturer's instructions; set timer for 12 minutes. Allow 10 to 15 minutes for pressure to build.

Step 2

Release pressure using the natural-release method according to manufacturer's instructions, about 15 minutes. Release remaining pressure using the quick-release method, about 5 minutes.

Step 3

Preheat the oven to 200 degrees F (95 degrees C).

Step 4

Unlock and remove the lid. Transfer sausages to a plate and potatoes into a large bowl. Break up the potatoes with a potato masher and stir in 1/4 cup butter until melted and incorporated Slowly mix in whipping cream until desired consistency

is reached. Season with salt and pepper. Place mashed potatoes in the oven to keep warm.
Step 5
Wash out the pressure cooker pot. Return to the cooker and select Saute function. Melt 2 tablespoons butter. Cook sausages in the melted butter until browned on each side, 2 to 3 minutes. Transfer sausages to an oven-safe container and keep warm in the oven.
Step 6
Deglaze Instant Pot with 2 tablespoons of beef broth, stirring and scraping the bottom of the pot to remove any brown bits. Add sliced onion and saute until onion is softened and browned, 3 to 4 minutes.
Step 7
Whisk flour and 2 tablespoons broth together in a small bowl to create a slurry. Pour in remaining broth and whisk until well combined. Pour broth mixture into the pot and cook, whisking frequently, until gravy begins to thicken. Stir in browning sauce and season with salt and pepper.
Step 8
Place a scoop of mashed potatoes onto a plate, top with two bangers and onion gravy, and serve immediately.
Nutrition Facts
Per Serving:
870.6 calories; protein 44.7g 90% DV; carbohydrates 58.7g 19% DV; fat 50.6g 78% DV; cholesterol 194.2mg 65% DV; sodium 1532.9mg 61% DV.

Instant Pot Garlic-Herb Chicken and Rice

prep: 15 mins cook: 30 mins additional: 25 mins total: 1 hr 10 mins
Servings: 6
Ingredients
- 1 ½ cups uncooked white rice
- 1 tablespoon lemon juice
- 2 teaspoons chili powder, divided
- 1 tcaspoon salt
- ½ teaspoon ground black pepper
- 6 eaches chicken thighs
- 1 tablespoon vegetable oil
- 2 tablespoons butter
- 1 large onion, chopped
- 1 ½ tablespoons minced garlic
- ½ tablespoon dried oregano
- ½ tablespoon ground thyme
- ½ tablespoon dried parsley
- 1 teaspoon paprika, or to taste
- 2 cups chickcn broth
- 1 pinch salt and ground black pepper to taste
- 1 tablespoon grated Parmesan cheese, or to taste
- 1 teaspoon chopped fresh parsley, or to taste

Directions
Step 1
Rinse rice in a colander until the water runs clear. Let soak while you prepare the rest.
Step 2
Mix lemon juice, 1 teaspoon chili powder, 1 teaspoon salt, and 1/2 teaspoon black pepper together in a small bowl. Rub over chicken thighs.
Step 3

Turn on a multi-functional pressure cooker (such as Instant Pot) and select Saute function. Add the oil when pot is hot. Add seasoned chicken to the pot and sear, 2 to 3 minutes on each side. Remove and set aside.

Step 4

Melt butter in the pot, add onion, and cook until soft and translucent, 5 to 7 minutes. Add garlic and cook until fragrant, about 30 seconds, watching carefully as it will brown fast. Add oregano, thyme, dried parsley, paprika, and remaining 1 teaspoon chili powder. Mix well. Add rice and roast, 2 to 3 minutes. Pour in chicken broth, making sure to scrape the bottom of the pot completely. Season with salt and pepper to taste. Add chicken in a single layer; add any liquid made while resting.

Step 5

Close and lock the lid. Select high pressure according to manufacturer's instructions; set timer for 8 minutes. Allow 10 to 15 minutes for pressure to build.

Step 6

Release pressure using the natural-release method according to manufacturer's instructions for 10 minutes. Release any remaining pressure carefully using the quick-release method according to manufacturer's instructions, about 5 minutes. Unlock and remove the lid. Let rest for an additional 10 minutes.

Step 7

Sprinkle with Parmesan cheese and parsley when serving.

Cook's Notes:

You can use chicken drumsticks instead of thighs, if preferred.

Watch the garlic carefully when cooking. I sometimes turn the pot off or lift it up when cooking minced garlic.

Nutrition Facts

Per Serving:

439.7 calories; protein 23.8g 48% DV; carbohydrates 41.6g 13% DV; fat 19g 29% DV; cholesterol 83.9mg 28% DV; sodium 918.9mg 37% DV.

Instant Pot Korean BBQ Tacos

prep: 15 mins cook: 1 hr additional: 5 mins total: 1 hr 20 mins
Servings: 12

Ingredients

- 1 tablespoon butter
- ½ onion, sliced
- 10 cloves garlic, diced
- 1 (1 inch) piece ginger root, peeled and grated
- 2 tablespoons seasoned rice vinegar
- 3 pounds chuck roast, trimmed and cut into several large pieces
- ½ cup brown sugar
- ⅓ cup soy sauce
- 1 tablespoon sesame oil
- 1 tablespoon chile-garlic paste
- 1 pinch salt and ground black pepper to taste

Directions

Step 1

Turn on a multi-functional pressure cooker (such as Instant Pot) and select Saute function. Add butter and onion and cook until soft, about 5 minutes. Add garlic and ginger and cook until aromatic, about 30 seconds more. Deglaze the pot with

vinegar and scrape the bottom. Add chuck pieces, brown sugar, soy sauce, sesame oil, chile-garlic paste, salt, and black pepper.
Step 2
Close and lock the lid; be sure vent is closed. Select high pressure according to manufacturer's instructions; set timer for 45 minutes. Allow 10 to 15 minutes for pressure to build.
Step 3
Release pressure carefully using the quick-release method according to manufacturer's instructions, about 5 minutes. Unlock and remove the lid. Remove beef and shred.

Nutrition Facts
Per Serving:
241 calories; protein 13.9g 28% DV; carbohydrates 12.5g 4% DV; fat 15g 23% DV; cholesterol 54.1mg 18% DV; sodium 516.1mg 21% DV.

Instant Pot Eggs and Soldiers

prep: 5 mins cook: 10 mins additional: 5 mins total: 20 mins
Servings: 4

Ingredients
- 4 large eggs
- 1 pinch salt and ground black pepper to taste
- 4 slices bread
- 4 teaspoons unsalted butter

Directions
Step 1
Turn on a multi-functional pressure cooker (such as Instant Pot), and pour 1 cup of water into the pot. Add a trivet or egg rack, and place the eggs on it. Close and lock the lid. Set the pressure valve to Sealing. Select high pressure according to manufacturer's instructions; set timer for 3 minutes. Allow 5 to 10 minutes for pressure to build.
Step 2
Cover the valve loosely with a kitchen towel. Use a wooden spoon or tongs to move the valve from Sealing to Venting to release pressure immediately. Unlock and remove the lid. Remove the eggs to a bowl of ice water for 2 minutes to stop cooking.
Step 3
Toast bread and spread with butter. Cut into strips.
Step 4
Drain the eggs and tap the tops with a spoon to crack the upper shell. Remove the tops. Season with salt and pepper, and serve with the toast sticks for dipping.
Cook's Note:
The pressure must be released immediately when timer stops. If you don't do this, the eggs will continue to cook from the residual heat in the pot, and they will not be perfectly cooked with runny yolks and firm egg whites. I just throw a kitchen towel on top of the valve when first releasing the pressure to keep the steam from going everywhere.
Nutrition Facts

Per Serving:
171.7 calories; protein 8.2g 17% DV; carbohydrates 13g 4% DV; fat 9.6g 15% DV; cholesterol 196.1mg 65% DV; sodium 279.5mg 11% DV.

Gluten-Free Instant Pot Beef Stroganoff

prep: 10 mins cook: 25 mins additional: 10 mins total: 45 mins
Servings: 4

Ingredients

- 1 serving cooking spray
- 1 pound ground beef
- ½ cup chopped onion
- 2 cloves garlic, minced
- 4 cups low-sodium beef broth (such as Swanson)
- 1 (10.5 ounce) can gluten-free cream of mushroom soup (such as Great Value™)
- 1 teaspoon salt
- ½ teaspoon ground black pepper
- 1 (12 ounce) package gluten-free spiral pasta (such as Ronzoni)
- 1 cup sour cream

Directions
Step 1
Turn on a multi-functional pressure cooker (such as Instant Pot) and select Saute function. Coat the pot with cooking spray. Cook and stir beef, onion, and garlic until beef is browned, about 5 minutes. Add beef broth, cream of mushroom soup, salt, and pepper; stir together. Stir in pasta.
Step 2
Close and lock the lid. Select low pressure according to manufacturer's instructions; set timer for 8 minutes. Allow 10 to 15 minutes for pressure to build.
Step 3
Allow steam to release naturally for 5 minutes. Carefully switch to the quick-release method for remaining pressure. Unlock and remove the lid. Add sour cream and mix in thoroughly. Serve immediately.
Cook's Note:
Substitute ground turkey for the ground beef if desired.
Nutrition Facts
Per Serving:
741.2 calories; protein 33.2g 66% DV; carbohydrates 77.8g 25% DV; fat 32.8g 51% DV; cholesterol 94.1mg 31% DV; sodium 1231.2mg 49% DV.

Instant Pot Chicken and Tortilla Soup

prep: 5 mins cook: 20 mins additional: 20 mins total: 45 mins
Servings: 6

Ingredients

- 1 (32 fluid ounce) container chicken broth
- 1 (15 ounce) can fire-roasted diced tomatoes
- 1 ½ cups frozen corn
- 1 onion, chopped
- ½ cup cauliflower rice
- ¼ cup quinoa
- 3 cloves garlic
- 2 teaspoons chili powder
- 3 teaspoons ground cumin
- 1 teaspoon paprika
- 1 teaspoon salt
- ½ teaspoon ground black pepper
- 1 pound chicken breast
- 3 tablespoons vegetable oil for frying
- 2 (8 inch) corn tortillas, cut into bite-sized strips

Directions
Step 1
Combine chicken broth, tomatoes, corn, onion, cauliflower rice, quinoa, garlic, chili powder, cumin, paprika, salt, and pepper in a multi-functional pressure cooker (such as Instant Pot). Add chicken breast. Close and lock the lid. Select high pressure according to manufacturer's instructions; set timer for 7 minutes. Allow 10 to 15 minutes for pressure to build.
Step 2
Meanwhile heat oil in a skillet over moderately high heat. Add tortilla strips and cook until golden, about 1 minute. Remove with a slotted spoon and drain on paper towels.
Step 3
Release pressure using the natural-release method according to manufacturer's instructions, about 15 minutes. Release remaining pressure carefully using the quick-release method according to manufacturer's instructions, about 5 minutes. Unlock and remove the lid. Remove chicken and shred or cut into bite-sized pieces.
Step 4
Return chicken to pot to warm. Ladle into soup bowls and top with fried tortilla strips.
Nutrition Facts
Per Serving:
227.5 calories; protein 20.1g 40% DV; carbohydrates 28.5g 9% DV; fat 4.1g 6% DV; cholesterol 42.7mg 14% DV; sodium 1345.4mg 54% DV.

Instant Pot Coconut Chicken Curry with Sweet Potato

prep: 10 mins cook: 25 mins additional: 5 mins total: 40 mins
Servings: 6
Ingredients

- 2 tablespoons grapeseed oil, divided
- 1 pound chicken tenders
- 1 teaspoon salt, divided
- 1 pinch ground black pepper
- ½ cup coarsely chopped onion
- ½ cup diced red bell pepper
- ½ cup diced green bell pepper
- 2 ½ teaspoons curry powder
- 1 (14 ounce) can coconut milk
- 1 medium sweet potato, peeled and diced
- ½ cup peeled and chopped carrots
- 1 tablespoon peanut butter

Directions
Step 1
Turn on a multi-functional pressure cooker (such as Instant Pot) and select Saute function. Once the pot is hot, add 1 tablespoon oil. Season chicken with 1/2 teaspoon salt and pepper. Add chicken to the pot and cook until no longer pink in the center, 5 to 7 minutes. Remove chicken and cover to keep warm. Add remaining 1 tablespoon oil to the pot and cook onion and bell peppers until softened, 3 to 5 minutes. Season with curry powder and remaining salt. Mix in coconut milk, sweet potatoes, and carrots. Bring to a boil.
Step 2
Hit cancel on Saute function. Close and lock the lid. Select high pressure according to manufacturer's instructions; set timer for 3 minutes. Allow 10 to 15 minutes for pressure to build.
Step 3
Dice cooked chicken while vegetables are cooking.
Step 4
Release pressure carefully using the quick-release method according to manufacturer's instructions, about 5 minutes. Unlock and remove the lid. Mix in chicken and peanut butter and serve.
Nutrition Facts
Per Serving:
320.2 calories; protein 18.9g 38% DV; carbohydrates 14.2g 5% DV; fat 21.9g 34% DV; cholesterol 43.1mg 14% DV; sodium 476.1mg 19% DV.

Texas Venison

prep: 25 mins cook: 15 mins additional: 20 mins total: 1 hr
Servings: 4

Ingredients

- 2 pounds venison steaks
- 1 ½ teaspoons seasoned salt, divided (see Note)
- 1 cup all-purpose flour
- 4 tablespoons vegetable oil
- ½ teaspoon ground cumin
- ½ cup onion, halved and sliced
- 2 cube (blank)s beef bouillon cubes
- ½ teaspoon dried Mexican oregano
- 1 bay leaf
- 2 peppers dried red chile peppers
- 2 cups water

Directions
Step 1
Lightly season the venison steaks with 1/2 teaspoon of Papa's Seasoning Salt (see below). Cut the steaks into bite-sized pieces. Mix the flour with 1 teaspoon of Papa's salt; reserve 1 tablespoon of the flour mixture and set aside. Toss the cubed meat in the seasoned flour.
Step 2
Heat the oil in the pressure cooker or a skillet over medium-high heat. Add the meat cubes in batches and cook until richly browned on all sides. Remove the meat and set aside.
Step 3
Reduce the heat to medium, and stir the reserved tablespoon of seasoned flour and the ground cumin into the pan drippings. Cook and stir until the flour has lost its raw smell and is lightly browned, about 5 minutes. Add the sliced onion and cook, stirring often, until the onion has softened, about 5 minutes.
Step 4
Return the meat to the pan, along with the beef bouillon cubes, Mexican oregano, bay leaf, and chile peppers (remove the stems, but leave them whole). Pour in the water and seal the pressure cooker, turning the heat up to high.
Step 5
Bring the pressure up to high and reduce the heat to maintain the pressure. Cook at high pressure for 15 minutes. Turn off the heat and let the pressure drop naturally. Remove the lid. Remove the chile peppers and bay leaf; squeeze the pulp from the peppers, returning the pulp to the pan and discarding the skins and the bay leaf. Taste and adjust the seasonings.
Cook's Notes
You may substitute 1 teaspoon cayenne pepper for the dried red chiles. This recipe is fairly hot; you can use milder chiles or reduce the amount of cayenne, if desired.
Slow Cooker Method:
Follow recipe as above, but transfer the meat to a slow cooker after browning the meat and cooking the flour mixture (roux). Cook until the meat is tender, 3-4 hours on high or 6-8 hours on low.
Nutrition Facts
Per Serving:

492.5 calories; protein 50g 100% DV; carbohydrates 26.3g 9% DV; fat 19.4g 30% DV; cholesterol 171.5mg 57% DV; sodium 868.8mg 35% DV.

Instant Pot Shrimp Curry

prep: 10 mins cook: 30 mins additional: 15 mins total: 55 mins
Servings: 4

Ingredients
- 2 tablespoons coconut oil
- 1 tablespoon black mustard seeds
- 1 sprig fresh curry leaves
- 1 teaspoon ginger-garlic paste
- ¼ teaspoon fenugreek powder
- 1 small onion, sliced
- 1 medium tomato, chopped
- 1 teaspoon salt
- ¼ teaspoon turmeric powder
- 2 tablespoons water
- 2 tablespoons Kashmiri red chili powder
- 1 ½ tablespoons coriander powder
- ¼ teaspoon cumin powder
- 2 tablespoons tamarind pulp
- 2 ¼ cups water, divided
- 12 ounces raw medium-large shrimp, peeled and deveined
- 2 tablespoons coconut cream

Directions
Step 1
Turn on a multi-functional pressure cooker (such as Instant Pot) and select the Saute function. Add oil, mustard seeds, curry leaves, ginger-garlic paste, and fenugreek powder. Stir well to prevent burning or sticking to the pot. Add onion and tomato, along with salt and turmeric. Saute until onions are translucent, 3 to 4 minutes.
Step 2
Meanwhile, combine 2 tablespoons water, Kashmiri red chili powder, coriander, and cumin into a paste in a small bowl. Add spice paste to the onions in the pot and stir well for 1 minute. Add tamarind and 1/4 cup water and stir to prevent burning or sticking to the pot. Cook and stir until oil starts separating out, 3 to 5 minutes. Add 2 cups water and cover the pot with the lid. Simmer 2 minutes more on Saute mode.
Step 3
Add shrimp and stir well. Close and lock the lid. Select high pressure and set the timer for 3 minutes. Allow about 10 minutes for pressure to build.
Step 4
Release pressure using the natural-release method according to manufacturer's instructions for 10 minutes. Release remaining pressure carefully using the quick-release method according to manufacturer's instructions, about 5 minutes. Unlock and remove the lid.
Step 5
Select Saute mode again and stir coconut cream into the curry. Simmer until thickened, 3 to 4 minutes. Season with salt, if desired.

Cook's Note:

You can replace the Kashmiri red chili powder (bright color and less heat) with paprika. You can get them at any Indian grocery store.
Nutrition Facts
Per Serving:
217.6 calories; protein 16.2g 32% DV; carbohydrates 12.4g 4% DV; fat 12g 19% DV; cholesterol 127.7mg 43% DV; sodium 818.2mg 33% DV.

Instant Pot Salmon Piccata

prep: 10 mins cook: 15 mins additional: 10 mins total: 35 mins
Servings: 2
Ingredients
- 2 (5 ounce) salmon fillets
- 1 pinch salt and freshly ground black pepper to taste
- ½ cup water
- 1 tablespoon butter
- 1 tablespoon minced garlic
- 1 cup chicken broth, divided
- 1 ½ teaspoons cornstarch
- ¼ cup heavy cream
- 2 tablespoons lemon juice
- 1 teaspoon onion-herb seasoning (such as Savory Spice Capitol Hill)
- 2 tablespoons capers

Directions
Step 1
Place salmon on a steamer rack; season with salt and pepper. Place rack inside a multi-functional electric pressure cooker (such as Instant Pot). Fill liner with water. Close and lock the lid. Select Steam setting; cook for 15 minutes.
Step 2
Combine butter and garlic in a skillet over medium heat. Saute until garlic is golden and fragrant, 2 to 3 minutes. Pour in chicken broth; reserve 2 tablespoons. Mix cornstarch with the reserved broth and stir into the skillet. Add heavy cream, lemon juice, and onion-herb seasoning. Stir sauce to combine.
Step 3
Release pressure using the natural-release method according to manufacturer's instructions, 10 to 20 minutes. Place each salmon fillet on a dinner plate. Spoon sauce on top and sprinkle with capers.
Nutrition Facts
Per Serving:
383.1 calories; protein 32g 64% DV; carbohydrates 5.5g 2% DV; fat 25.5g 39% DV; cholesterol 122mg 41% DV; sodium 1102.7mg 44% DV.

Instant Pot Mushroom and Soba Noodle Stir-Fry

prep: 15 mins cook: 20 mins additional: 5 mins total: 40 mins
Servings: 4

Ingredients

- 2 tablespoons olive oil
- 1 tablespoon sesame oil
- 5 cloves garlic, minced
- 1 cup sliced cremini mushrooms
- 2 medium carrots, julienned
- 1 medium red bell pepper, seeded and chopped
- 2 tablespoons tamari
- 1 (10.5 ounce) package dried soba noodles
- 2 ¼ cups water, or as needed
- 1 green onion, finely chopped

Directions
Step 1
Turn on a multi-functional pressure cooker (such as Instant Pot) and select Saute function. When Instant Pot displays hot, add olive oil and sesame oil. Add garlic and cook until fragrant, about 1 minute. Stir in mushrooms, carrots, and pepper; toss to combine. Cook until softened, 2 to 3 minutes.
Step 2
Push vegetables to the outside of the pot, forming an empty circle in the center. Add tamari and soba noodles to the pot and enough water so noodles are just covered. Cancel Saute mode.
Step 3
Close and lock the lid. Select high pressure according to manufacturer's instructions; set timer for 6 minutes. Allow 10 to 15 minutes for pressure to build.
Step 4
Release pressure carefully using the quick-release method according to manufacturer's instructions, about 5 minutes. Unlock and remove the lid. Mix sauce, noodles and vegetables together using tongs. Sprinkle with chopped green onion and serve immediately.
Nutrition Facts
Per Serving:
381.6 calories; protein 13.6g 27% DV; carbohydrates 63.1g 20% DV; fat 10.9g 17% DV; cholesterolmg; sodium 1129mg 45% DV.

Instant Pot Vegetarian White "Chicken" Chili

prep: 15 mins cook: 25 mins additional: 10 mins total: 50 mins
Servings: 6
Ingredients

- 2 tablespoons olive oil
- 1 onion, finely chopped
- 2 eaches jalapeno peppers, seeded and finely chopped
- 1 green bell pepper, finely chopped
- 2 cloves garlic, finely chopped
- 1 (12 ounce) package artificial chicken pieces (such as Quorn™)
- 4 cups vegetable broth
- 2 (16 ounce) cans pinto beans, rinsed and drained
- 1 (16 ounce) package frozen cauliflower florets
- 1 cup frozen sweet corn
- 1 teaspoon dried oregano
- 1 teaspoon ground cumin
- 1 teaspoon ground black pepper
- 1 pinch salt to taste
- ½ cup sour cream
- 2 tablespoons chopped fresh cilantro, or to taste

Directions
Step 1
Turn on a multi-functional pressure cooker (such as Instant Pot), select Saute function, and add olive oil. Add onion, jalapeno peppers, bell pepper, and garlic to hot oil; saute until onions begins to soften, about 3 minutes. Add artificial chicken pieces and saute for another 3 minutes.
Step 2
Add vegetable broth, pinto beans, frozen cauliflower, frozen corn, oregano, cumin, pepper, and salt. Close and lock the lid. Select Soup function and set timer for 15 minutes.
Step 3
Release pressure using the natural-release method according to manufacturer's instructions, for 5 minutes. Release remaining pressure carefully using the quick-release method according to manufacturer's instructions, about 5 minutes. Unlock and remove the lid.
Step 4
Stir in sour cream. Ladle into bowls and top with fresh cilantro.
Nutrition Facts
Per Serving:
350.6 calories; protein 19.6g 39% DV; carbohydrates 45.6g 15% DV; fat 12g 19% DV; cholesterol 8.4mg 3% DV; sodium 1043.4mg 42% DV.

Make-Ahead Instant Pot Cauliflower Rice

prep: 5 mins cook: 15 mins additional: 5 mins total: 25 mins
Servings: 8

Ingredients

- 1 (4 pound) cauliflower, cut into large florets

Directions
Step 1
Pour 1 cup water into a multi-functional pressure cooker (such as Instant Pot) and set a trivet inside. Place a steamer basket on top of the trivet and place cauliflower inside.
Step 2
Close and lock the lid. Select high pressure according to manufacturer's instructions; set timer for 1 minute. Allow 10 to 15 minutes for pressure to build.
Step 3
Release pressure carefully using the quick-release method according to manufacturer's instructions, about 2 minutes. Transfer cauliflower to a bowl of ice water to stop the cooking.
Step 4
Use a food processor to pulse cauliflower into rice-sized pieces. Place riced cauliflower in a colander and press to remove excess water.
Step 5
Scoop individual servings of cauliflower rice into freezer-safe zip-top bags and freeze.
Nutrition Facts
Per Serving:
56.8 calories; protein 4.5g 9% DV; carbohydrates 12g 4% DV; fat 0.2g; cholesterolmg; sodium 68.1mg 3% DV.

My World Famous Pressure Cooker Chinese Ribs

prep: 15 mins cook: 25 mins total: 40 mins
Servings: 4

Ingredients

- 3 tablespoons paprika
- 1 tablespoon garlic powder
- ½ teaspoon ground black pepper
- ½ teaspoon salt
- 6 ½ pounds pork ribs
- 2 tablespoons vegetable oil
- 3 cups water
- ¾ cup ketchup
- ¼ cup brown sugar
- ¼ cup Chinese vinegar
- 1 teaspoon Worcestershire sauce

Directions
Step 1
Mix paprika, garlic powder, black pepper, and salt in a resealable plastic bag. Place ribs in bag, seal the bag, and shake thoroughly until ribs are completely coated. Remove ribs from bag and discard dry rub.
Step 2
Heat oil in a wok over medium-high heat. Cook ribs in hot oil until browned all over, 3 to 4 minutes per side.
Step 3
Stir water, ketchup, brown sugar, vinegar, and Worcestershire sauce together in a pressure cooker. Add browned ribs to pressure cooker. Lock the lid onto the pressure cooker, bring the cooker up to pressure, and reduce heat to medium.
Step 4
Cook ribs over medium heat for 15 minutes. Remove from heat and release pressure according to manufacturer's directions.
Nutrition:
The nutrition data for this recipe includes the full amount of the dry rub ingredients. The actual amount of the rub consumed will vary.
Nutrition Facts
Per Serving:
1468.7 calories; protein 95.6g 191% DV; carbohydrates 31.9g 10% DV; fat 105.3g 162% DV; cholesterol 389.9mg 130% DV; sodium 1121mg 45% DV.

Instant Pot Tuna Puttanesca

prep: 10 mins cook: 30 mins additional: 5 mins total: 45 mins
Servings: 2

Ingredients
-
- 1 ½ teaspoons olive oil
- ¼ cup diced onion
- 2 cloves garlic, minced
- ½ (24 ounce) jar traditional spaghetti sauce (such as Barilla)
- ½ cup fire-roasted diced tomatoes
- ¼ cup vegetable broth
- 1 (6 ounce) frozen tuna steak
- 1 (8 ounce) package spaghetti
- 2 tablespoons sliced black olives, drained
- 1 tablespoon capers, drained and chopped
- 1 teaspoon anchovy paste
- ½ teaspoon herbes de Provence
- ¼ teaspoon cayenne pepper

Directions
Step 1
Turn on a multi-functional pressure cooker (such as Instant Pot) and select Saute function. Heat olive oil in the pot. Add onion and garlic; saute until softened and fragrant, about 4 minutes.
Step 2
Add spaghetti sauce, diced tomatoes, and broth; stir to combine. Nestle tuna steak into the middle of the sauce. Cancel Saute function. Close and lock the lid. Select high pressure according to manufacturer's instructions; set timer for 12 minutes. Allow 10 to 15 minutes for pressure to build.

Step 3
Meanwhile, bring a large pot of lightly salted water to a boil. Cook spaghetti in the boiling water, stirring occasionally, until tender yet firm to the bite, about 12 minutes. Drain and set aside.
Step 4
Release pressure carefully using the quick-release method according to manufacturer's instructions, about 5 minutes. Flake tuna apart with a fork. Add olives, capers, anchovy paste, herbes de Provence, and cayenne. Stir to combine and serve over hot cooked spaghetti.
Nutrition Facts
Per Serving:
735.3 calories; protein 39.2g 78% DV; carbohydrates 115.2g 37% DV; fat 11.7g 18% DV; cholesterol 43.2mg 14% DV; sodium 1454.1mg 58% DV.

Instant Pot Keto Chicken Curry

prep: 10 mins cook: 25 mins additional: 5 mins total: 40 mins
Servings: 4

Ingredients

- 3 tablespoons ghee (clarified butter)
- 1 tablespoon tomato paste
- 1 tablespoon red curry paste
- 2 (5 ounce) boneless skinless chicken breasts, cut into 1-inch pieces
- ½ cup chopped onion
- 2 cloves garlic, minced
- ½ cup coconut milk
- ⅓ cup heavy whipping cream
- 1 teaspoon yellow curry powder
- ½ teaspoon garam masala
- ½ teaspoon ground turmeric
- 1 pinch stevia-erythritol sweetener (such as Truvia)

Directions
Step 1
Turn on a multi-functional pressure cooker (such as Instant Pot) and select Saute function. Allow pot to heat up, then add ghee, tomato paste, and curry paste. Cook and stir until paste starts to sizzle, about 3 minutes. Stir in chicken, onion, and garlic and saute for 3 to 5 minutes. Stir in coconut milk and cream until combined. Cancel Saute function.
Step 2
Close and lock the lid. Select high pressure according to manufacturer's instructions; set timer for 7 minutes. Allow 10 to 15 minutes for pressure to build.
Step 3
Release pressure carefully using the quick-release method according to manufacturer's instructions, about 5 minutes. Unlock and remove the lid. Stir in curry powder, garam masala, turmeric, and sweetener.
Nutrition Facts
Per Serving:
305.8 calories; protein 17.6g 35% DV; carbohydrates 5.8g 2% DV; fat 26.9g 41% DV; cholesterol 91.9mg 31% DV; sodium 152.5mg 6% DV.

Instant Pot Chicken Congee

prep: 10 mins cook: 50 mins additional: 15 minstotal: 1 hr 15 mins
Servings: 6
Ingredients

- 1 cup uncooked short-grain white rice
- 1 tablespoon olive oil
- 14 ounces boneless, skinless chicken breast
- 6 cups chicken broth
- 1 (2 inch) piece grated fresh ginger
- 1 ear fresh corn, husked
- 1 pinch salt and ground black pepper to taste
- Topping:
- 3 eaches spring onions, sliced
- 6 teaspoons black sesame seeds
- 6 teaspoons spicy chili crisp sauce

Directions
Step 1
Rinse rice under cold running water until the water runs clear. Set aside.
Step 2
Turn on a multi-functional pressure cooker (such as Instant Pot) and select Saute function. Heat oil and brown chicken on all sides, about 8 minutes, making sure each side is browned before flipping. Add a few tablespoons of chicken broth to the Instant Pot and scrape off any browned bits from the bottom with a wooden spatula. Turn off Saute function. Add drained rice, ginger, and remaining broth.
Step 3
Cut the kernels from the corn cob and break cob into 3 pieces. Add corn kernels and cob pieces to the pot. Close and seal the lid. Select Porridge function and set timer for 30 minutes. Allow 10 to 15 minutes for pressure to build.
Step 4
Release pressure using the natural-release method according to manufacturer's instructions, about 15 minutes. Open the lid and discard the corn cob pieces. Remove chicken breast. Shred chicken with two forks and return to the congee. Season with salt and pepper and mix well.
Step 5
Divide congee amongst 6 bowls. Top each bowl with equal amounts of sliced spring onions, sesame seeds, and chili crisp.
Nutrition Facts
Per Serving:
299.4 calories; protein 18.3g 37% DV; carbohydrates 32.5g 11% DV; fat 9.7g 15% DV; cholesterol 43.7mg 15% DV; sodium 1272.2mg 51% DV.

Grandma's Creamy Chicken in the Instant Pot

prep: 15 mins cook: 35 mins additional: 10 mins total: 1 hr
Servings: 8
Ingredients

- 3 eaches onions, coarsely chopped
- 1 stick butter, melted
- ¼ cup chicken broth
- 2 tablespoons minced garlic
- 1 tablespoon poultry seasoning
- 1 teaspoon salt
- 1 teaspoon ground black pepper
- ½ teaspoon paprika
- ½ teaspoon smoked paprika
- 4 eaches skinless, boneless chicken breasts, cut in half
- 2 tablespoons all-purpose flour
- 1 (24 ounce) container sour cream

Directions
Step 1
Place onions into the bottom of a multi-functional pressure cooker (such as Instant Pot). Pour melted butter and broth on top.
Step 2
Mix garlic, poultry seasoning, salt, pepper, paprika, and smoked paprika together in a small bowl. Stir into onions. Place chicken on top of the onions.
Step 3
Close and lock the lid. Select high pressure according to manufacturer's instructions; set timer for 9 minutes. Allow 10 to 15 minutes for pressure to build.
Step 4
Release pressure using the natural-release method according to manufacturer's instructions, 10 to 40 minutes.
Step 5
Transfer chicken and onions to a plate. Select Saute function to bring juices to a simmer, about 5 minutes.
Step 6
Sift flour into the pot and stir until no lumps remain and sauce has thickened a bit, about 5 minutes. Add sour cream by the spoonful, stirring to incorporate. Cancel Saute function. Return chicken and onions to the pot. Select Warm function to heat through, about 5 minutes. Serve.
Cook's Notes:
You can use white or yellow onions. If you chop them into large pieces, they hold up better.
Feel free to substitute any spice or seasoning blend for poultry seasoning.
Make sure to release pressure naturally; do not rush, as this will make the chicken rubbery and tough.
Nutrition Facts
Per Serving:
394.1 calories; protein 16g 32% DV; carbohydrates 14.4g 5% DV; fat 30.9g 48% DV; cholesterol 100.4mg 34% DV; sodium 486.1mg 19% DV.

Easy Instant Pot Baby Back Ribs

prep: 20 mins cook: 50 mins additional: 20 mins total: 1 hr 30 mins
Servings: 6

Ingredients

- 1 cup water
- ½ cup apple cider vinegar
- 1 tablespoon liquid smoke flavoring
- 1 rack baby back pork ribs
- 1 pinch salt and freshly ground black pepper to taste
- 1 (12 ounce) bottle barbeque sauce, divided

Directions
Step 1
Combine water, vinegar, and liquid smoke in the pot of a multi-functional pressure cooker (such as Instant Pot). Place rack in the bottom of the pot.
Step 2
Season baby back pork ribs with salt and pepper on both sides. Cut rack in half. Place ribs in a teepee formation onto the rack. Pour a little barbeque sauce onto each half and let run down the sides. Close and lock the lid.
Step 3
Select Meat setting according to manufacturer's instructions; set timer for 30 minutes. Allow 10 to 15 minutes for pressure to build.
Step 4
Wait 15 minutes before releasing pressure carefully using the quick-release method according to manufacturer's instructions, about 5 minutes. Unlock and remove the lid.
Step 5
Set an oven rack about 6 inches from the heat source and preheat the oven's broiler. Line a baking pan with aluminum foil. Place ribs onto the prepared baking pan and slather with barbeque sauce.
Step 6
Cook under the broiler for 5 minutes. Remove and immediately add more sauce.
Nutrition Facts
Per Serving:
291.4 calories; protein 12g 24% DV; carbohydrates 20.5g 7% DV; fat 17.1g 26% DV; cholesterol 58.4mg 20% DV; sodium 704.7mg 28% DV.

Instant Pot Sushi Rice

prep: 20 mins cook: 15 mins additional: 20 mins total: 55 mins
Servings: 6

Ingredients

- 1 cup Japanese sushi-style rice
- 1 (2 inch) piece kombu (Japanese dried kelp)
- 1 ¼ cups water
- 3 tablespoons Japanese rice wine

- 1 tablespoon hon-mirin (Japanese mirin)
- ¾ tablespoon white sugar
- ½ teaspoon sea salt

Directions
Step 1
Place rice in the insert of a multi-functional pressure cooker (such as Instant Pot). Add enough water to cover and rinse rice, mixing it in a circular motion. Strain through a sieve. Repeat until water comes out clear, about 5 rinses total. Spread drained rice on a clean cloth to dry out for 10 to 15 minutes.
Step 2
Clean kombu gently with a damp towel but do not remove the white powder, which is important for the umami flavor.
Step 3
Break off a small piece of the kombu and put into a small saucepan. Add the rest of the kombu to the Instant Pot. Add rice and 1 1/4 cups water. Close and lock the lid. Select high pressure according to manufacturer's instructions; set timer for 2 minutes. Allow 10 to 15 minutes for pressure to build.
Step 4
Add rice wine, hon-mirin, sugar, and sea salt to the saucepan. Heat over low heat until sugar and salt have dissolved; do not boil.
Step 5
Release pressure using the natural-release method according to manufacturer's instructions, about 8 minutes. Release any additional pressure carefully using the quick-release method. Unlock and remove the lid.
Step 6
Gently scrape rice into a glass or ceramic bowl using a rice paddle; remove and discard kombu. Remove and discard the smaller kombo piece from the vinegar mixture. Sprinkle vinegar mixture over rice and cut it into the rice with the rice paddle. Stir in vinegar mixture until well incorporated and no lumps of rice remain. Allow to cool to room temperature. You can use a piece of cardboard to fan the rice and speed up cooling.
Nutrition Facts
Per Serving:
145.7 calories; protein 2.4g 5% DV; carbohydrates 30.1g 10% DV; fat 0.2g; cholesterolmg; sodium 198.2mg 8% DV.

Instant Pot Linguine with Pesto and Peas

prep: 5 mins cook: 20 mins additional: 10 mins total: 35 mins
Servings: 4
Ingredients

- 5 ½ cups water
- 1 (16 ounce) package linguine pasta
- 1 teaspoon salt
- 1 teaspoon dried parsley
- ½ teaspoon ground black pepper
- 4 cups frozen peas, thawed and drained
- 2 cups ricotta cheese
- ½ cup pesto sauce
- 4 tablespoons grated Parmesan cheese

Directions
Step 1
Combine water, pasta, salt, parsley, and pepper in a multi-functional pressure cooker (such as Instant Pot). Seal lid. Select high pressure according to manufacturer's instructions; set timer for 2 minutes. Allow 10 to 15 minutes for pressure to build.
Step 2
Release pressure carefully using the quick-release method according to manufacturer's instructions, about 5 minutes. Unlock and remove the lid. Stir in peas, ricotta cheese, pesto, and Parmesan. Seal lid again and cook on high pressure for 1 minute, allowing 5 to 10 minutes for pressure to build.
Step 3
Release pressure carefully using the quick-release method, about 5 minutes.
Nutrition Facts
Per Serving:
578.9 calories; protein 22.5g 45% DV; carbohydrates 84g 27% DV; fat 18.2g 28% DV; cholesterol 14.4mg 5% DV; sodium 912mg 37% DV.

Instant Pot Galbi (Korean-Style Short Ribs)

prep: 20 mins cook: 55 mins additional: 1 hr 10 mins total: 2 hrs 25 mins
Servings: 6
Ingredients

- 3 pounds beef short ribs
- 1 Asian pear - peeled, cored, and coarsely chopped
- 1 small onion, chopped
- 4 cloves garlic, chopped
- ½ tablespoon peeled and coarsely chopped fresh ginger
- 1 cup low-sodium soy sauce, divided
- ¼ cup rice wine
- ¼ cup water
- ¼ cup brown sugar

- 2 tablespoons sesame oil, divided
- ½ teaspoon ground black pepper
- 2 eaches carrots, peeled and cut in chunks
- 5 eaches radishes, peeled and cut into chunks
- ¼ cup white sugar
- ½ bunch green onions, chopped, or to taste
- 1 tablespoon sesame seeds, or to taste

Directions
Step 1
Soak ribs in a large bowl of water for 1 hour.
Step 2
Meanwhile, combine Asian pear, onion, garlic, and ginger in a blender or food processor; puree until smooth. Transfer mixture to a mixing bowl. Add 3/4 cup soy sauce, rice wine, water, brown sugar, 1 tablespoon sesame oil, and pepper and mix to create the sauce.
Step 3
Drain ribs and dry them well. Trim off excess fat. Place ribs in a multi-functional pressure cooker (such as Instant Pot) and add carrots and radishes. Pour Asian pear sauce on top. Close and lock the lid. Select Meat function according to

manufacturer's instructions; set timer for 35 minutes. Allow 10 to 15 minutes for pressure to build.
Step 4
Release pressure using the natural-release method according to manufacturer's instructions, 10 to 40 minutes. Unlock and remove the lid. Transfer meat and vegetables to a plate and set aside.
Step 5
Select the Saute function on your Instant Pot. Stir in remaining soy sauce, remaining sesame oil, and white sugar. Cook, stirring occasionally, until sugar has melted and sauce has thickened, about 10 minutes. Return ribs and vegetables to the pot to get nice and saucy.
Step 6
Garnish ribs and vegetables with green onions and sesame seeds.
Nutrition Facts
Per Serving:
656.6 calories; protein 25.2g 50% DV; carbohydrates 30.6g 10% DV; fat 47.1g 73% DV; cholesterol 93.2mg 31% DV; sodium 1588.5mg 64% DV.

Pressure Cooker Butter Beans with Beer and Bacon

prep: 15 mins cook: 40 mins additional: 8 hrs 10 mins total: 9 hrs 5 mins
Servings: 8
Ingredients

- 1 pound dried large lima beans (butter beans)
- 1 pound bacon
- 4 cups water, or more as needed
- 1 (12 fluid ounce) can or bottle beer
- ½ teaspoon ground cumin
- ½ jalapeno pepper, seeded and minced
- 1 clove garlic, minced

Directions
Step 1
Place beans into a large container and cover with several inches of cool water; let stand 8 hours to overnight.
Step 2
Place bacon in the open pressure cooker and cook over medium-high heat, turning occasionally, until evenly browned, about 10 minutes. Drain bacon slices on paper towels and remove pressure cooker from heat, reserving the bacon grease in the pressure cooker to cool, about 10 minutes.
Step 3
Stir 4 cups water into cooled bacon grease; add beer and cumin.
Step 4
Drain and rinse the soaked beans and add to the water mixture in the pressure cooker.
Step 5

Place the lid on the pressure cooker and secure tightly. Cook beans according to manufacturers' instructions for 15 psi over medium-high heat, about 30 minutes; release the pressure.
Step 6
Stir jalapeno pepper and garlic into beans. Crumple bacon over beans.
Step 7
Close pressure cooker again and bring to 15 psi over medium heat and immediately turn off heat. Remove pressure cooker from heat and allow pressure naturally decrease to 0 psi.
Cook's Note:
You can add a 1/2 teaspoon of kosher salt or 1/2 Lawry's(R) seasoning salt but not both; the beans may become too salty if not careful.
Nutrition Facts
Per Serving:
313 calories; protein 19.3g 39% DV; carbohydrates 38g 12% DV; fat 8.2g 13% DV; cholesterol 20.5mg 7% DV; sodium 446.1mg 18% DV.

Instant Pot Split Pea Soup

prep: 20 mins cook: 40 mins additional: 15 mins total: 1 hr 15 mins
Servings: 6
Ingredients

- 2 tablespoons butter
- 1 tablespoon olive oil
- 1 onion, diced
- 3 stalks celery, diced
- 2 leaf (blank)s bay leaves
- ½ teaspoon dried thyme
- 3 carrot, (7-1/2")s carrots, chopped
- 6 slices bacon, chopped
- 4 cloves garlic, minced
- ½ teaspoon salt
- ¼ teaspoon ground black pepper
- 6 cups chicken broth
- 1 pound green split peas, rinsed and sorted

Directions
Step 1
Turn on a multi-functional pressure cooker (such as Instant Pot) and select Saute function. Let warm up and add butter and olive oil. Add onion, celery, bay leaves, and thyme. Cook, stirring occasionally, until onion starts to turn translucent, about 5 minutes.
Step 2
Add carrots, bacon, garlic, salt, and pepper. Cook until fragrant, about 1 minute. Add broth and bring to a simmer. Stir in split peas. Close and lock the lid; set release knob to Sealing position.
Step 3
Select Manual/Pressure Cook setting according to manufacturer's instructions; set timer for 18 minutes. Allow 10 to 15 minutes for pressure to build.
Step 4
Release pressure using the natural-release method according to manufacturer's instructions, about 15 minutes. Turn steam release knob to Venting and use quick-release function for the remaining pressure. Carefully open lid. Remove bay leaves. Taste and adjust seasonings as desired.

Cook's Note:
For a vegetarian version, substitute vegetable broth for the chicken broth and 1 teaspoon liquid smoke for the bacon.
Nutrition Facts
Per Serving:
408.4 calories; protein 24g 48% DV; carbohydrates 53.6g 17% DV; fat 11.6g 18% DV; cholesterol 26.3mg 9% DV; sodium 1649.9mg 66% DV.

Pressure Cooker Mashed Potatoes

prep: 15 mins cook: 30 mins additional: 10 mins total: 55 mins
Servings: 6
Ingredients
- 3 cups cold water, or as needed
- 3 ½ pounds russet potatoes, peeled and sliced 3/4 inch thick
- ¼ cup butter
- ½ cup whole milk
- 2 teaspoons kosher salt
- ½ teaspoon white pepper

Directions
Step 1
Bring water to a boil in a pressure cooker over high heat. When water is boiling, add potatoes. Seal lid and bring cooker up to high pressure. Reduce heat to low, maintaining high pressure, and cook for 30 minutes.
Step 2
Use quick-release method to lower the pressure. Drain potatoes and return them to pressure cooker. Add butter and milk and cover pressure cooker with lid for 5 minutes, allowing the heat from the potatoes to melt the butter and warm the milk.
Step 3
Remove lid. Season with kosher salt and white pepper, and use a hand masher to mash potatoes until lumps are mostly gone. Transfer to a bowl and serve hot.
Cook's Note:
These potatoes are great as is, but are absolutely wonderful with some of these alterations. Try mixing in a bit of prepared horseradish or chopped green onions. Or substitute cream cheese for some of the milk. I also like using a mixture of 1/2 cup sour cream, 1 tablespoon lemon juice, and 1 teaspoon dill (mixed 30 minutes beforehand for flavors to mingle) in place of the milk.
Nutrition Facts
Per Serving:
289.6 calories; protein 6.4g 13% DV; carbohydrates 48.9g 16% DV; fat 8.5g 13% DV; cholesterol 22.4mg 8% DV; sodium 719.4mg 29% DV.

Instant Pot Shrimp and Broccoli

prep: 10 mins cook: 15 mins additional: 5 mins total: 30 mins
Servings: 4
Ingredients

- ¼ cup reduced-sodium soy sauce
- 2 tablespoons oyster sauce

- 1 tablespoon rice vinegar
- 2 teaspoons sesame oil
- 1 teaspoon brown sugar
- 1 teaspoon Sriracha sauce
- 1 teaspoon minced garlic
- 1 pound raw peeled and deveined shrimp
- 2 tablespoons cornstarch
- 2 tablespoons cold water
- 2 cups fresh broccoli florets
- 2 eaches green onions, chopped
- 1 tablespoon toasted sesame seeds

Directions
Step 1
Whisk soy sauce, oyster sauce, rice vinegar, sesame oil, brown sugar, Sriracha sauce, and garlic in a small bowl until smooth.
Step 2
Pour sauce into a multi-functional pressure cooker (such as Instant Pot). Stir in shrimp. Close and lock the lid. Select high pressure according to manufacturer's instructions; set timer for 0 minutes. Allow 10 minutes for pressure to build.
Step 3
Meanwhile, whisk cornstarch and cold water together until smooth.
Step 4
Release pressure carefully using the quick-release method according to manufacturer's instructions, about 2 minutes. Unlock and remove the lid. Stir in cornstarch slurry and broccoli. Select Saute function and cook until sauce thickens and broccoli is crisp-tender, about 2 minutes.
Step 5
Garnish shrimp and broccoli with green onions and sesame seeds.
Cook's Note:
I prefer my broccoli bright green and crisp tender, which is why I add it in the end. If you prefer more well done broccoli, add it in with the shrimp prior to bringing the pot up to pressure.
Nutrition Facts
Per Serving:
172.7 calories; protein 21.2g 42% DV; carbohydrates 10.8g 4% DV; fat 4.6g 7% DV; cholesterol 172.6mg 58% DV; sodium 858.2mg 34% DV.

Instant Pot Khichdi

prep: 10 mins cook: 35 mins additional: 50 mins total: 1 hr 35 mins
Servings: 6

Ingredients

- 1 cup brown basmati rice
- ½ cup whole green mung beans
- ¼ cup split yellow dal
- 1 ½ teaspoons cumin seeds
- 1 ½ teaspoons brown mustard seeds
- 8 tablespoons ghee, divided
- 1 shallot, sliced
- 1 tablespoon minced fresh ginger root
- 1 tablespoon goda masala
- 1 teaspoon ground turmeric
- 1 teaspoon ground black pepper
- ½ teaspoon salt
- 6 cups water

Directions
Step 1
Rinse rice and mung beans. Cover with water and soak for 15 minutes. Rinse split yellow dal and add to the rice and mung beans to soak for 15 minutes. Drain and set aside.
Step 2
Turn on a multi-functional pressure cooker (such as Instant Pot) and select Saute function. Saute cumin and mustard seeds in 2 tablespoons ghee until fragrant, about 2 minutes. Add shallot and ginger and cook until shallot is tender and translucent, about 5 minutes. Add the drained rice and legumes; stir to combine. Turn off Saute function.
Step 3
Stir in goda masala, turmeric, pepper, and salt. Add water; stir well. Close and lock the lid. Select high pressure and set timer for 18 minutes according to manufacturer's instructions. Allow 10 to 15 minutes for pressure to build.
Step 4
Allow pressure to release naturally for 15 minutes. Manually release any remaining pressure, 5 to 10 minutes more. Stir khichdi and divide between 6 bowls. Top each with 1 tablespoon of remaining ghee.
Nutrition Facts
Per Serving:
351.4 calories; protein 9.1g 18% DV; carbohydrates 40.2g 13% DV; fat 18.6g 29% DV; cholesterol 43.7mg 15% DV; sodium 206.2mg 8% DV.

Instant Pot Moroccan Chicken Tagine

prep: 25 mins cook: 35 mins additional: 3 hrs 10 mins total: 4 hrs 10 mins
Servings: 6

Ingredients
- 2 tablespoons minced fresh garlic
- 1 ¼ teaspoons paprika
- ¾ teaspoon ground ginger
- ¾ teaspoon ground turmeric
- ⅛ teaspoon saffron powder
- 1 ½ pounds skinless, boneless chicken breasts, cut into bite-sized pieces
- 1 preserved lemon
- 2 tablespoons extra-virgin olive oil
- 2 tablespoons butter
- 2 medium red onions, sliced
- 1 cinnamon stick
- 1 cup pitted and halved Mediterranean olives
- 1 cup chicken broth
- 1 tablespoon chopped fresh flat-leaf parsley
- 1 tablespoon chopped fresh cilantro

Directions
Step 1
Combine garlic, paprika, ginger, turmeric, and saffron in a large bowl. Add chicken pieces and mix until coated with spices. Cover and refrigerate, 3 to 4 hours or overnight.
Step 2

Cut preserved lemon into quarters. Remove pulp from the peel and remove seeds from pulp. Mince pulp and set aside. Cut lemon peel into strips and set aside.

Step 3

Turn on a multi-functional pressure cooker (such as Instant Pot) and select Saute function. Heat olive oil and butter in the cooker; add chicken. Cook chicken until browned, about 3 minutes per side. Transfer chicken to a plate, reserving drippings in the pot.

Step 4

Place onions and lemon pulp into the hot pot and cook, stirring occasionally, until onions have softened, about 5 minutes. Add cinnamon stick, place chicken on top, and scatter olives and lemon peel over the chicken. Pour in chicken broth. Close and lock the lid. Select high pressure according to manufacturer's instructions; set timer for 10 minutes. Allow 10 to 15 minutes for pressure to build.

Step 5

Release pressure using the natural-release method according to manufacturer's instructions, about 10 minutes. Unlock and remove the lid carefully, turning it away from you. Transfer contents to a large serving bowl. Sprinkle with parsley and cilantro and serve immediately.

Cook's Note:

You can use any skinless, boneless cut of chicken that you'd like.

Nutrition Facts

Per Serving:

257.2 calories; protein 24.6g 49% DV; carbohydrates 8.7g 3% DV; fat 13.8g 21% DV; cholesterol 75.8mg 25% DV; sodium 2538.4mg 102% DV.

Instant Pot Chili

prep: 20 mins cook: 30 mins additional: 10 mins total: 1 hr

Servings: 8

Ingredients

- 1 tablespoon vegetable oil
- 1 pound lean ground beef
- 1 large onion, diced
- 4 cloves garlic, crushed
- ½ teaspoon salt
- ¼ cup chili powder
- 1 tablespoon ground cumin
- 1 teaspoon dried oregano
- 1 ½ cups water
- 4 (15 ounce) cans kidney beans, drained
- 1 (28 ounce) can crushed tomatoes
- 2 tablespoons tomato paste

Directions

Step 1

Turn on a multi-functional pressure cooker (such as Instant Pot) and select Saute function. Add ground beef. Cook and stir until browned and crumbly, 5 to 7 minutes. Drain and discard grease. Transfer cooked beef to a separate container.

Step 2

Pour oil into the Instant Pot and select Saute function. Add onion, garlic, and salt. Cook until softened, 5 to 7 minutes. Make a hole in the center of the mixture and add chili powder, cumin, and oregano. Let spices sit for 30 seconds, then stir into the onion. Return cooked beef to the pot and add water. Stir, being sure to scrape any browned bits from the bottom.

Step 3
Stir beans, crushed tomatoes, and tomato paste into the beef mixture. Close and
lock the lid. Select Chili function and set the timer for 10 minutes. Allow 10 to 15
minutes for pressure to build.
Step 4
Release pressure using the natural-release method according to manufacturer's
instructions, 10 to 40 minutes. Unlock and remove the lid.
Cook's Notes:
Use any kind of canned beans you like. You can substitute tomato sauce for the
crushed tomatoes.
To save preparation time, I do the following the night before: Brown the beef,
drain, and place in a covered container in the refrigerator. Chop the onion and
place in a covered container in the refrigerator. Measure the spices and place in a
covered container.
Nutrition Facts
Per Serving:
362.6 calories; protein 25.1g 50% DV; carbohydrates 45.1g 15% DV; fat 10.6g
16% DV; cholesterol 39.5mg 13% DV; sodium 837.6mg 34% DV.

Instant Pot Beef Burritos

prep: 15 mins cook: 25 mins additional: 5 mins total: 45 mins
Servings: 8
Ingredients

- 1 pound 85% lean ground beef
- 1 teaspoon kosher salt
- ½ teaspoon ground black pepper
- 1 small onion, diced
- 1 tablespoon olive oil
- 1 cup uncooked long grain rice
- 1 (15 ounce) can black beans, drained and rinsed
- 1 (14.5 ounce) can fire-roasted diced tomatoes, drained
- 1 (14.5 ounce) can vegetable broth
- 2 (1 ounce) packets taco seasoning
- ¼ cup chopped cilantro, or to taste
- 8 (10 inch) burrito-size tortillas, or as needed
- 2 cups shredded Mexican cheese blend
- 2 eaches tomatoes, diced, or more to taste
- 1 avocado, diced, or more to taste
- ¼ cup sour cream, or to taste
- 2 eaches green onions, chopped, or to taste

Directions
Step 1
Turn on a multi-functional pressure cooker (such as Instant Pot) and select Saute
function; if available, select "more" option. Add ground beef, salt, and pepper.
Cook and stir beef until browned and crumbly, 5 to 7 minutes. Add onion and cook
until starting to soften, 1 to 3 minutes more. Add olive oil and rice. Cook and stir
until some grains start to turn golden brown, about 2 minutes. Stir in beans,
tomatoes, broth, and taco seasoning.
Step 2

Close and lock the lid. Select high pressure according to manufacturer's instructions; set timer for 7 minutes. Allow 10 to 15 minutes for pressure to build.
Step 3
Release pressure carefully using the quick-release method according to manufacturer's instructions, about 5 minutes. Unlock and remove the lid. Fluff burrito bowl filling with a fork and add cilantro.
Step 4
Serve filling in tortillas with Mexican cheese blend. Garnish with fresh tomatoes, avocado, sour cream, and green onions.
Cook's Note:
Substitute chicken broth for the vegetable broth if preferred.
Nutrition Facts
Per Serving:
684.5 calories; protein 29.6g 59% DV; carbohydrates 77g 25% DV; fat 27.7g 43% DV; cholesterol 67.7mg 23% DV; sodium 1804.8mg 72% DV.

Instant Pot Acorn Squash Stuffed with Italian Sausage

prep: 15 mins cook: 20 mins additional: 15 mins total: 50 mins
Servings: 2
Ingredients
- 1 tablespoon olive oil
- ½ pound Italian pork sausage
- ½ small onion, diced
- ¼ cup diced red bell pepper
- ½ cup marinara sauce, divided
- ½ cup shredded mozzarella cheese
- 2 tablespoons panko bread crumbs
- 2 cloves garlic, crushed
- ¼ teaspoon oregano
- ¼ teaspoon freshly ground black pepper
- 1 acorn squash, halved and seeded
- 1 cup water

Directions
Step 1
Turn on a multi-functional pressure cooker (such as Instant Pot), add olive oil, and select Saute function. Add sausage, onion, and bell pepper. Cook until sausage is browned and crumbly, 5 to 7 minutes. Add 1/4 cup marinara sauce, 1/4 cup mozzarella cheese, bread crumbs, garlic, oregano, and black pepper. Stir until well combined.
Step 2
Transfer mixture to a bowl; drain and discard any excess grease.
Step 3
Stuff each squash half with sausage mixture. Place trivet inside the pressure cooker pot and add water. Place stuffed squash halves on the trivet. Close and lock the lid; be sure vent is sealed. Select high pressure according to manufacturer's instructions; set timer for 4 minutes. Allow 10 to 15 minutes for pressure to build.
Step 4

Release pressure using the natural-release method for 7 minutes. Release remaining pressure carefully using the quick-release method according to manufacturer's instructions, about 5 minutes. Unlock and remove the lid.
Step 5
Carefully transfer squash halves to a serving plate and top with remaining marinara sauce and mozzarella cheese.
Nutrition Facts
Per Serving:
589.7 calories; protein 26.2g 52% DV; carbohydrates 47.5g 15% DV; fat 34.8g 54% DV; cholesterol 63.8mg 21% DV; sodium 1418.9mg 57% DV.

Electric Pressure Cooker Chicken and Dumplings

prep: 15 mins cook: 50 mins additional: 15 mins total: 1 hr 20 mins
Servings: 8
Ingredients
- 1 large chicken breast
- 1 tablespoon paprika
- 2 teaspoons garlic powder
- 1 ½ teaspoons salt
- 1 ½ teaspoons ground black pepper
- 4 cups chicken stock, divided
- 2 (12 ounce) packages frozen dumpling wrappers
- 2 cups cream of chicken soup
- 1 ½ cups frozen peas and carrots
- 1 pinch salt and ground black pepper to taste

Directions
Step 1
Season chicken with paprika, garlic powder, salt, and black pepper. Combine chicken breast and 2 cups stock in an electric pressure cooker (such as Instant Pot). Close and lock the lid. Turn on the pressure cooker and select Stew function. Set timer for 25 minutes. Allow time for pressure to build, 5 to 10 minutes.
Step 2
Release pressure carefully using the quick-release method according to manufacturer's instructions, about 5 minutes. Unlock and remove the lid. Transfer chicken to a cutting board. Set pressure cooker to Saute function and allow broth to come to a boil. Shred chicken meat using 2 forks.
Step 3
Add frozen dumpling wrappers to the broth, stirring often to prevent sticking together. Add shredded chicken, cream of chicken soup, and remaining stock to the pressure cooker. Add salt and pepper to taste. Close and lock the lid and set pressure cooker to Stew function. Set timer for 10 minutes. Allow time for pressure to build, 5 to 10 minutes.
Step 4
Release pressure using the natural-release method according to manufacturer's instructions, 10 to 40 minutes. Unlock lid; stir in peas and carrots and allow to sit until warmed through, 1 to 2 minutes.
Cook's Note:
If you're not in a hurry, it's best to allow the spices to sit on the chicken for 24 hours.

Instant Pot Brunswick Stew

prep: 10 mins cook: 45 mins additional: 10 mins total: 1 hr 5 mins
Servings: 6
Ingredients

- 2 (14.5 ounce) cans whole peeled tomatoes
- 2 eaches russet potatoes, peeled and diced, or more to taste
- 2 cups chicken broth
- 1 cup diced onion
- ¼ cup Worcestershire sauce
- ¼ cup apple cider vinegar
- 3 tablespoons ketchup
- ½ teaspoon red pepper flakes, or to taste
- 2 (6 ounce) bone-in chicken breast halves
- ¼ teaspoon seasoned salt, or to taste
- 1 dash ground thyme
- 1 pinch ground black pepper to taste
- 1 (10 ounce) package frozen corn
- 1 (10 ounce) package frozen baby lima beans
- 1 (10 ounce) package frozen sliced okra
- ¾ cup shredded cooked pork, or to taste

Directions
Step 1
Combine tomatoes, potatoes, chicken broth, onion, Worcestershire sauce, vinegar, ketchup, and red pepper flakes in the pot of a multi-functional pressure cooker (such as Instant Pot). Lay chicken breasts on top; add seasoned salt, thyme, and black pepper. Close and lock the lid. Select high pressure according to manufacturer's instructions; set timer for 20 minutes. Allow 10 to 15 minutes for pressure to build.
Step 2
Release pressure carefully using the quick-release method according to manufacturer's instructions, about 5 minutes. Unlock and remove lid.
Step 3
Remove chicken from pot and set on a plate to cool. Place corn, lima beans, and okra into the pot and stir to combine.
Step 4
Remove skin from chicken, shred the meat off the bones, and return to the pot. Add pork. Seal cooker; select low pressure and cook until vegetables are heated through, about 15 minutes. Release pressure carefully using the quick-release method according to manufacturer's instructions, about 5 minutes. Unlock and remove lid.
Nutrition Facts
Per Serving:
312.2 calories; protein 24g 48% DV; carbohydrates 44.8g 15% DV; fat 4.7g 7% DV; cholesterol 48.9mg 16% DV; sodium 941.5mg 38% DV.

Pressure Cooker Goat Curry

prep: 30 mins cook: 1 hr 2 mins total: 1 hr 32 mins
Servings: 8
Ingredients

- ¼ cup vegetable oil, divided
- 2 large onions, thinly sliced
- 2 large tomatoes, peeled and diced
- 2 tablespoons garlic paste
- 1 tablespoon ginger paste
- 2 ½ pounds goat meat, cubed
- 1 cup water
- 1 potato, cubed
- 1 large carrot, sliced
- 2 teaspoons garam masala
- 2 teaspoons ground coriander
- 1 teaspoon ground cumin
- ½ teaspoon ground turmeric
- 2 teaspoons salt, or to taste
- ½ teaspoon ground red chile pepper

Directions
Step 1
Heat 2 tablespoons oil in an electric pressure cooker on the "Sear" setting. Add onions; cook and stir until golden brown, 10 to 15 minutes.
Step 2
Transfer onions to a food processor; grind into a paste. Remove to a bowl.
Step 3
Combine tomatoes, garlic paste, and ginger paste in the food processor; puree until smooth.
Step 4
Heat remaining 2 tablespoons oil in the pressure cooker using the "Sear" setting. Add onion paste; cook, stirring constantly, until browned, about 2 minutes. Stir in the tomato mixture. Add goat meat, water, potato, carrot, garam masala, coriander, cumin, turmeric, salt, and red chile pepper.
Step 5
Close pressure cooker and seal according to manufacturer's instructions. Set the timer for 50 minutes at high pressure. Release pressure using the natural-release method according to manufacturer's instructions.
Nutrition Facts
Per Serving:
254.9 calories; protein 25.8g 52% DV; carbohydrates 13g 4% DV; fat 10.1g 16% DV; cholesterol 66.4mg 22% DV; sodium 800.4mg 32% DV.

Instant Pot Crispy Barbecue Chicken Wings

prep: 5 mins cook: 40 mins additional: 5 mins total: 50 mins
Servings: 4
Ingredients

- 1 cup water
- 2 ½ pounds frozen chicken wings
- 1 cup barbeque sauce
- 1 tablespoon butter, melted

Directions
Step 1
Turn on a multi-functional pressure cooker (such as Instant Pot) and select manual function. Place the trivet in the pot and add the water. Place wings on the trivet. Close and lock the lid and seal the vent. Select high pressure according to manufacturer's instructions; set timer for 12 minutes. Allow 20 to 25 minutes for pressure to build.
Step 2
Release pressure carefully using the quick-release method according to manufacturer's instructions, about 5 minutes. Unlock and remove the lid.
Step 3
Set an oven rack about 6 inches from the heat source and preheat the oven's broiler. Line a jelly roll pan with aluminum foil.
Step 4
Remove wings from pressure cooker and pat dry with paper towels. Mix barbecue sauce and melted butter together in a bowl. Place wings on the prepared pan and baste with barbecue sauce mixture.
Step 5
Cook wings under the hot broiler, turning once, until desired crispness is reached, 5 to 15 minutes.
Cook's Notes:
If you use thawed wings, allow 10 to 15 minutes for pressure to build.
If you use an air fryer, set it for 400 degrees F and cook for 20 minutes turning halfway to ensure even browning until desired caramelization and crispness. Baste again with barbecue sauce if desired.
Nutrition Facts
Per Serving:
348.4 calories; protein 14.1g 28% DV; carbohydrates 30.4g 10% DV; fat 18.5g 28% DV; cholesterol 63.5mg 21% DV; sodium 948mg 38% DV.

Instant Pot Pineapple-Coconut-Lime Rice

prep: 10 mins cook: 3 mins additional: 20 mins total: 33 mins
Servings: 4
Ingredients

- 1 ½ cups uncooked long-grain white rice
- 1 cup water
- 1 (8 ounce) can crushed pineapple, undrained
- ¾ cup coconut milk
- ¼ teaspoon red pepper flakes
- 1 lime, zested and juiced

Directions
Step 1
Rinse rice well until water runs clear. Place drained rice in the pot of electric pressure cooker (such as Instant Pot). Add water, pineapple chunks and juice, coconut milk, and red pepper flakes. Place the lid on the pot and lock in place.
Step 2

Turn the cooker on and choose the "Manual" setting and high pressure. Set the timer for 3 minutes. Allow pressure to release naturally after the cooking time has ended, about 20 minutes. Stir in lime zest and juice.
Nutrition Facts
Per Serving:
371.8 calories; protein 6.1g 12% DV; carbohydrates 65.9g 21% DV; fat 9.6g 15% DV; cholesterolmg; sodium 11.4mg 1% DV.

Instant Pot Shepherd's Pie with Potatoes and Yams

prep: 20 mins cook: 45 mins additional: 10 mins total: 1 hr 15 mins
Servings: 10
Ingredients

- 1 cup low-sodium chicken broth
- 1 large yam, chopped
- 1 large russet potato, chopped
- 1 teaspoon Himalayan pink salt
- ½ cup milk
- 3 tablespoons butter
- Meat Filling:
- 1 tablespoon vegetable oil
- ½ onion, chopped
- 2 cloves garlic, mashed
- 1 ⅛ pounds ground beef
- 1 pinch salt and ground black pepper to taste
- 6 medium (blank)s mushrooms, sliced
- 1 cup frozen corn
- 1 cup frozen green peas
- 1 crown broccoli, diced
- 1 carrot, chopped
- 1 stalk celery, chopped
- 1 (.87 ounce) package low-sodium gravy mix
- 1 tablespoon water, or as needed
- ½ cup shredded Cheddar cheese

Directions
Step 1
Pour chicken broth into a multi-functional electric pressure cooker. Place a steamer rack into the pot. Add yam and potato; sprinkle pink salt on top. Close and lock the lid. Turn valve to Seal. Select high pressure according to manufacturer's instructions; set timer for 8 minutes. Allow 10 to 15 minutes for pressure to build.
Step 2
Release pressure carefully using the quick-release method according to manufacturer's instructions, about 5 minutes. Unlock and remove lid. Remove yam, potato, and rack. Strain liquid into a glass measuring cup and reserve. Return yam and potato to pot. Add milk and butter; mash using a potato masher until smooth. Scrape mashed potato topping into a bowl using a silicone spatula.
Step 3
Preheat the oven to 350 degrees F (175 degrees C).
Step 4
Select Saute function on the pressure cooker. Heat oil on high mode. Add onion and garlic; saute until slightly tender, 1 to 2 minutes. Add ground beef, salt, and pepper. Cook and stir until filling is well combined, 2 to 3 minutes. Add mushrooms; saute until starting to soften, about 1 minute.
Step 5

Stir corn, peas, broccoli, carrot, and celery into the pot with the filling. Pour in reserved potato liquid. Close and lock the lid. Set pot to Manual function. Select low pressure according to manufacturer's instructions; set timer for 3 minutes. Allow 5 to 10 minutes for pressure to build.

Step 6
Release pressure carefully using the quick-release method according to manufacturer's instructions, about 5 minutes. Unlock and remove lid. Strain out excess liquid and discard; return filling to pot. Set pot to Saute mode.

Step 7
Dissolve gravy mix in just enough water to dissolve the powder; add to the filling in the pot. Cook and stir until gravy thickens, about 2 minutes. Transfer filling to a baking dish and cover with the mashed topping. Sprinkle Cheddar cheese on top.

Step 8
Bake in the preheated oven until cheese is melted, about 10 minutes.

Step 9
Set oven rack about 6 inches from the heat source and preheat the oven's broiler. Broil shepherd's pie until top is browned, 3 to 5 minutes. Let sit for 5 minutes before serving.

Cook's Notes:
Ground turkey can be substituted for the ground beef.
Substitute salt and pepper with steak seasoning (such as The Keg(R)), if desired.
Broiling is optional.

Nutrition Facts
Per Serving:
308.6 calories; protein 14g 28% DV; carbohydrates 29.8g 10% DV; fat 15g 23% DV; cholesterol 47.1mg 16% DV; sodium 467mg 19% DV.

Instant Pot Beef Burritos

prep: 15 mins cook: 25 mins additional: 5 mins total: 45 mins
Servings: 8
Ingredients

- 1 pound 85% lean ground beef
- 1 teaspoon kosher salt
- ½ teaspoon ground black pepper
- 1 small onion, diced
- 1 tablespoon olive oil
- 1 cup uncooked long grain rice
- 1 (15 ounce) can black beans, drained and rinsed
- 1 (14.5 ounce) can fire-roasted diced tomatoes, drained
- 1 (14.5 ounce) can vegetable broth
- 2 (1 ounce) packets taco seasoning
- ¼ cup chopped cilantro, or to taste
- 8 (10 inch) burrito-size tortillas, or as needed
- 2 cups shredded Mexican cheese blend
- 2 eaches tomatoes, diced, or more to taste
- 1 avocado, diced, or more to taste
- ¼ cup sour cream, or to taste
- 2 eaches green onions, chopped, or to taste

Directions

Step 1
Turn on a multi-functional pressure cooker (such as Instant Pot) and select Saute function; if available, select "more" option. Add ground beef, salt, and pepper. Cook and stir beef until browned and crumbly, 5 to 7 minutes. Add onion and cook until starting to soften, 1 to 3 minutes more. Add olive oil and rice. Cook and stir until some grains start to turn golden brown, about 2 minutes. Stir in beans, tomatoes, broth, and taco seasoning.

Step 2
Close and lock the lid. Select high pressure according to manufacturer's instructions; set timer for 7 minutes. Allow 10 to 15 minutes for pressure to build.

Step 3
Release pressure carefully using the quick-release method according to manufacturer's instructions, about 5 minutes. Unlock and remove the lid. Fluff burrito bowl filling with a fork and add cilantro.

Step 4
Serve filling in tortillas with Mexican cheese blend. Garnish with fresh tomatoes, avocado, sour cream, and green onions.

Cook's Note:
Substitute chicken broth for the vegetable broth if preferred.

Nutrition Facts
Per Serving:
684.5 calories; protein 29.6g 59% DV; carbohydrates 77g 25% DV; fat 27.7g 43% DV; cholesterol 67.7mg 23% DV; sodium 1804.8mg 72% DV.

Instant Pot Acorn Squash Stuffed with Italian Sausage

prep: 15 mins cook: 20 mins additional: 15 mins total: 50 mins
Servings: 2
Ingredients

- 1 tablespoon olive oil
- ½ pound Italian pork sausage
- ½ small onion, diced
- ¼ cup diced red bell pepper
- ½ cup marinara sauce, divided
- ½ cup shredded mozzarella cheese
- 2 tablespoons panko bread crumbs
- 2 cloves garlic, crushed
- ¼ teaspoon oregano
- ¼ teaspoon freshly ground black pepper
- 1 acorn squash, halved and seeded
- 1 cup water

Directions
Step 1
Turn on a multi-functional pressure cooker (such as Instant Pot), add olive oil, and select Saute function. Add sausage, onion, and bell pepper. Cook until sausage is browned and crumbly, 5 to 7 minutes. Add 1/4 cup marinara sauce, 1/4 cup mozzarella cheese, bread crumbs, garlic, oregano, and black pepper. Stir until well combined.

Step 2
Transfer mixture to a bowl; drain and discard any excess grease.

Step 3
Stuff each squash half with sausage mixture. Place trivet inside the pressure cooker
pot and add water. Place stuffed squash halves on the trivet. Close and lock the lid;
be sure vent is sealed. Select high pressure according to manufacturer's
instructions; set timer for 4 minutes. Allow 10 to 15 minutes for pressure to build.
Step 4
Release pressure using the natural-release method for 7 minutes. Release
remaining pressure carefully using the quick-release method according to
manufacturer's instructions, about 5 minutes. Unlock and remove the lid.
Step 5
Carefully transfer squash halves to a serving plate and top with remaining marinara
sauce and mozzarella cheese.
Nutrition Facts
Per Serving:
589.7 calories; protein 26.2g 52% DV; carbohydrates 47.5g 15% DV; fat 34.8g
54% DV; cholesterol 63.8mg 21% DV; sodium 1418.9mg 57% DV.

Electric Pressure Cooker Chicken and Dumplings

prep: 15 mins cook: 50 mins additional: 15 mins total: 1 hr 20 mins
Servings: 8
Ingredients
- 1 large chicken breast
- 1 tablespoon paprika
- 2 teaspoons garlic powder
- 1 ½ teaspoons salt
- 1 ½ teaspoons ground black pepper
- 4 cups chicken stock, divided
- 2 (12 ounce) packages frozen dumpling wrappers
- 2 cups cream of chicken soup
- 1 ½ cups frozen peas and carrots
- 1 pinch salt and ground black pepper to taste

Directions
Step 1
Season chicken with paprika, garlic powder, salt, and black pepper. Combine
chicken breast and 2 cups stock in an electric pressure cooker (such as Instant Pot).
Close and lock the lid. Turn on the pressure cooker and select Stew function. Set
timer for 25 minutes. Allow time for pressure to build, 5 to 10 minutes.
Step 2
Release pressure carefully using the quick-release method according to
manufacturer's instructions, about 5 minutes. Unlock and remove the lid. Transfer
chicken to a cutting board. Set pressure cooker to Saute function and allow broth
to come to a boil. Shred chicken meat using 2 forks.
Step 3
Add frozen dumpling wrappers to the broth, stirring often to prevent sticking
together. Add shredded chicken, cream of chicken soup, and remaining stock to
the pressure cooker. Add salt and pepper to taste. Close and lock the lid and set
pressure cooker to Stew function. Set timer for 10 minutes. Allow time for
pressure to build, 5 to 10 minutes.
Step 4

Release pressure using the natural-release method according to manufacturer's instructions, 10 to 40 minutes. Unlock lid; stir in peas and carrots and allow to sit until warmed through, 1 to 2 minutes.

Cook's Note:
If you're not in a hurry, it's best to allow the spices to sit on the chicken for 24 hours.

Nutrition Facts
Per Serving:
358.3 calories; protein 17.2g 34% DV; carbohydrates 58g 19% DV; fat 6.1g 9% DV; cholesterol 29.1mg 10% DV; sodium 1726.6mg 69% DV.

Instant Pot Brunswick Stew

prep: 10 mins cook: 45 mins additional: 10 mins total: 1 hr 5 mins
Servings: 6
Ingredients

- 2 (14.5 ounce) cans whole peeled tomatoes
- 2 eaches russet potatoes, peeled and diced, or more to taste
- 2 cups chicken broth
- 1 cup diced onion
- ¼ cup Worcestershire sauce
- ¼ cup apple cider vinegar
- 3 tablespoons ketchup
- ½ teaspoon red pepper flakes, or to taste
- 2 (6 ounce) bone-in chicken breast halves
- ¼ teaspoon seasoned salt, or to taste
- 1 dash ground thyme
- 1 pinch ground black pepper to taste
- 1 (10 ounce) package frozen corn
- 1 (10 ounce) package frozen baby lima beans
- 1 (10 ounce) package frozen sliced okra
- ¾ cup shredded cooked pork, or to taste

Directions
Step 1
Combine tomatoes, potatoes, chicken broth, onion, Worcestershire sauce, vinegar, ketchup, and red pepper flakes in the pot of a multi-functional pressure cooker (such as Instant Pot). Lay chicken breasts on top; add seasoned salt, thyme, and black pepper. Close and lock the lid. Select high pressure according to manufacturer's instructions; set timer for 20 minutes. Allow 10 to 15 minutes for pressure to build.
Step 2
Release pressure carefully using the quick-release method according to manufacturer's instructions, about 5 minutes. Unlock and remove lid.
Step 3
Remove chicken from pot and set on a plate to cool. Place corn, lima beans, and okra into the pot and stir to combine.
Step 4
Remove skin from chicken, shred the meat off the bones, and return to the pot. Add pork. Seal cooker; select low pressure and cook until vegetables are heated through, about 15 minutes. Release pressure carefully using the quick-release

method according to manufacturer's instructions, about 5 minutes. Unlock and remove lid.
Nutrition Facts
Per Serving:
312.2 calories; protein 24g 48% DV; carbohydrates 44.8g 15% DV; fat 4.7g 7% DV; cholesterol 48.9mg 16% DV; sodium 941.5mg 38% DV.

Pressure Cooker Goat Curry

prep: 30 mins cook: 1 hr 2 mins total: 1 hr 32 mins
Servings: 8
Ingredients

- ¼ cup vegetable oil, divided
- 2 large onions, thinly sliced
- 2 large tomatoes, peeled and diced
- 2 tablespoons garlic paste
- 1 tablespoon ginger paste
- 2 ½ pounds goat meat, cubed
- 1 cup water
- 1 potato, cubed
- 1 large carrot, sliced
- 2 teaspoons garam masala
- 2 teaspoons ground coriander
- 1 teaspoon ground cumin
- ½ teaspoon ground turmeric
- 2 teaspoons salt, or to taste
- ½ teaspoon ground red chile pepper

Directions
Step 1
Heat 2 tablespoons oil in an electric pressure cooker on the "Sear" setting. Add onions; cook and stir until golden brown, 10 to 15 minutes.
Step 2
Transfer onions to a food processor; grind into a paste. Remove to a bowl.
Step 3
Combine tomatoes, garlic paste, and ginger paste in the food processor; puree until smooth.
Step 4
Heat remaining 2 tablespoons oil in the pressure cooker using the "Sear" setting. Add onion paste; cook, stirring constantly, until browned, about 2 minutes. Stir in the tomato mixture. Add goat meat, water, potato, carrot, garam masala, coriander, cumin, turmeric, salt, and red chile pepper.
Step 5
Close pressure cooker and seal according to manufacturer's instructions. Set the timer for 50 minutes at high pressure. Release pressure using the natural-release method according to manufacturer's instructions.
Nutrition Facts
Per Serving:
254.9 calories; protein 25.8g 52% DV; carbohydrates 13g 4% DV; fat 10.1g 16% DV; cholesterol 66.4mg 22% DV; sodium 800.4mg 32% DV.

Instant Pot Creamy Cabbage Sausage Soup

prep: 15 mins cook: 30 mins additional: 5 mins total: 50 mins
Servings: 4
Ingredients

- 2 tablespoons butter
- 1 medium onion, chopped
- 1 pound sage pork sausage
- 1 cup water
- 1 teaspoon chicken soup base (such as Better than Bouillon)
- 1 russet potato, diced
- 2 cups chopped cabbage
- 1 pinch garlic salt, or to taste
- 1 pinch ground black pepper to taste
- 1 pinch ground allspice
- ½ cup milk, divided
- ½ cup half-and-half, divided
- 2 tablespoons all-purpose flour
- 2 teaspoons chopped fresh dill, or to taste

Directions
Step 1
Turn on a multi-functional pressure cooker (such as Instant Pot) and select Saute function. Add butter and stir until melted. Add onion; stir frequently until browned. Transfer to a plate. Add sausage and cook, breaking it into smaller crumbles with a wooden spoon, until browned, about 5 minutes.
Step 2
Add water and chicken soup base to the pot. Return onion to the pot. Stir in potato, cabbage, garlic salt, pepper, and allspice. Close and lock the lid. Select high pressure according to manufacturer's instructions; set timer for 8 minutes. Allow 10 to 15 minutes for pressure to build.
Step 3
Release pressure carefully using the quick-release method according to manufacturer's instructions, about 5 minutes. Unlock and remove the lid. Select Saute function again.
Step 4
Combine milk and half-and-half. Pour all but 3 tablespoons into the pot. Stir flour into the remaining milk mixture. Add flour mixture to the soup. Stir until heated through and adjust seasonings to taste. Garnish with fresh dill.
Nutrition Facts
Per Serving:
475.9 calories; protein 20g 40% DV; carbohydrates 21.6g 7% DV; fat 34.5g 53% DV; cholesterol 94.2mg 31% DV; sodium 1370.4mg 55% DV.

Instant Pot Chicken Noodle Soup

prep: 25 mins cook: 40 mins additional: 15 mins total: 1 hr 20 mins
Servings: 6
Ingredients

- 2 tablespoons salted butter
- 3 eaches carrots, or more to taste, peeled and sliced
- 3 stalks celery, or more to taste, chopped
- 1 medium onion, chopped
- 1 teaspoon ground thyme
- 1 teaspoon dried oregano
- 1 teaspoon salt, or to taste
- ½ teaspoon ground black pepper, or to taste
- 4 cups chicken broth
- 4 cups water
- 4 cubes chicken bouillon
- 2 eaches bay leaves
- 1 pound frozen skinless, boneless chicken breast halves
- 1 (8 ounce) package thin egg noodles
- 1 tablespoon dried parsley

Directions
Step 1
Turn on a multi-functional pressure cooker (such as Instant Pot), select Saute function, and add butter. Add carrots, celery, and onion to the melted butter; saute until soft, 3 to 5 minutes. Stir in thyme, oregano, salt, and pepper. Cancel Saute function.
Step 2
Stir in chicken broth, water, bouillon cubes, and bay leaves. Add frozen chicken breasts. Close and lock the lid. Select high pressure according to manufacturer's instructions; set timer for 12 minutes. Allow 10 to 15 minutes for pressure to build.
Step 3
Release pressure using the natural-release method according to manufacturer's instructions, 10 minutes. Switch to the quick-release method according to manufacturer's instructions, about 5 minutes. Unlock and remove the lid.
Step 4
Remove chicken from the pot. Carefully chop or shred the meat, and add back to the pot.
Step 5
Select Saute function and add egg noodles. Cook until noodles are tender yet firm to the bite, 8 to 10 minutes. Stir in dried parsley and serve.
Cook's Note:
If using unfrozen chicken, you could reduce the time from 12 to 10 minutes.
Nutrition Facts
Per Serving:
300.2 calories; protein 22.1g 44% DV; carbohydrates 34.5g 11% DV; fat 7.8g 12% DV; cholesterol 85mg 28% DV; sodium 2046mg 82% DV.

Instant Pot Red Beans and Rice with Sausage

prep: 10 mins cook: 1 hr additional: 20 mins total: 1 hr 30 mins
Servings: 12
Ingredients

- 1 tablespoon vegetable oil
- 14 ounces andouille sausage, sliced into rounds
- 1 medium onion, chopped
- 1 green bell pepper, chopped
- 3 stalks celery, chopped
- 1 clove garlic, minced
- 2 teaspoons Creole seasoning (such as Tony Chachere's)
- 1 teaspoon ground thyme
- 1 teaspoon oregano
- 1 pound dried red beans
- 4 cups chicken broth
- 1 tablespoon hot sauce (such as Louisiana)
- 1 bay leaf
- 4 cups hot cooked rice
- ¼ cup chopped fresh flat-leaf parsley
- 3 eaches green onions, chopped

Directions
Step 1
Turn on a multi-functional pressure cooker (such as Instant Pot) and select Saute function. Add oil and let heat about 30 seconds. Add sausage and cook for 5 minutes. Transfer to a plate using a slotted spoon and set sausage aside.
Step 2
Add onion, bell pepper, and celery to the Instant Pot and cook for 3 minutes. Add garlic, Creole seasoning, thyme, and oregano; cook 2 minutes more. Turn pot off.
Step 3
Add beans, broth, hot sauce, and bay leaf to the Instant Pot with the vegetables. Close and lock the lid. Select high pressure and set the timer for 30 minutes. Allow 10 minutes for pressure to build.
Step 4
Release pressure using the natural-release method according to manufacturer's instructions, 10 to 40 minutes. Unlock and remove the lid.
Step 5
Remove bay leaf from the pot and discard. Add reserved cooked sausage. Select Saute function. Cook, stirring frequently to mash some of the beans and thicken the mixture, for about 10 minutes. Turn off pot and let stand for 10 minutes.
Step 6
Serve beans over hot cooked rice garnished with parsley and green onions.
Nutrition Facts
Per Serving:
326.3 calories; protein 15.1g 30% DV; carbohydrates 41.2g 13% DV; fat 11.3g 17% DV; cholesterol 21mg 7% DV; sodium 815mg 33% DV.

Kelly's Pressure Cooker Beef Stew

prep: 25 mins cook: 15 mins additional: 15 mins total: 55 mins
Servings: 4
Ingredients

- 2 tablespoons vegetable oil
- ½ cup all-purpose flour
- 1 ¼ pounds beef stew meat, cubed
- 1 pinch salt and ground black pepper to taste
- 1 large onion, chopped
- 2 tablespoons white sugar
- 2 cups water
- 2 cubes beef bouillon
- 2 cloves garlic, minced
- 1 bay leaf
- 1 tablespoon dried parsley
- 1 tablespoon dried basil
- 4 eaches potatoes, peeled and cut into 2-inch pieces
- 2 cups peeled baby carrots

Directions
Step 1
Heat vegetable oil in a skillet over medium heat. Place flour in a resealable bag; drop in half the beef cubes and shake to coat. Shake off excess flour and add meat to pan. Repeat with remaining beef. Season meat with salt and pepper to taste.
Step 2
Stir onion into beef and cook, stirring often, until the meat is browned on all sides and onion is translucent, about 5 minutes. Sprinkle in sugar.
Step 3
Combine water, beef bouillon, garlic, bay leaf, parsley, and basil in a pressure cooker over medium-high heat. When bouillon cubes are dissolved, fit the pressure cooker's rack in the cooker (if it has one). Layer potatoes, carrots, and meat mixture in the pressure cooker, seasoning with salt and pepper to taste. Seal the lid and bring the cooker up to full pressure.

Step 4
Reduce heat to medium-low, maintaining full pressure, and cook for 8 minutes. Remove from heat. Let the pressure drop naturally, about 15 minutes before releasing lid. Transfer the meat and vegetables to a serving bowl and pour pan juices over meat and vegetables.
Nutrition Facts
Per Serving:
535.4 calories; protein 33.4g 67% DV; carbohydrates 65.2g 21% DV; fat 15.7g 24% DV; cholesterol 74.9mg 25% DV; sodium 557.3mg 22% DV.

Instant Pot Southern-Style Green Beans from a Can

prep: 10 mins cook: 30 mins additional: 5 mins total: 45 mins
Servings: 8
Ingredients

- 8 ounces thick cut bacon, cut into 1 inch pieces
- 1 cup diced yellow onion
- 2 tablespoons cider vinegar
- 4 (15 ounce) cans cut green beans, with liquid
- 2 teaspoons sea salt, or to taste
- ½ teaspoon black pepper
- 1 ½ pounds daikon (white radish), peeled and chopped

Directions
Step 1
Turn on a multi-functional pressure cooker (such as Instant Pot) and select Saute function. Add bacon and cook until almost crispy, about 8 minutes. Take your time cooking the bacon in order to render out all the fat. Add onions and cook, stirring frequently, until soft and translucent, about 3 minutes.
Step 2
Pour in vinegar and scrape up the brown bits from the bottom of the pot. Pour in beans and their liquid; season with salt and pepper. Stir in radishes. Close and lock the lid. Select high pressure according to manufacturer's instructions; set timer for 5 minutes. Allow 10 to 15 minutes for pressure to build.
Step 3
Release pressure carefully using the quick-release method according to manufacturer's instructions, about 5 minutes. Unlock and remove the lid.
Cook's Note:
Recipe Notes
If you want to make a smaller batch, scale down the ingredients but the cook time remains the same.
Nutrition Facts
Per Serving:
101.5 calories; protein 5g 10% DV; carbohydrates 11.3g 4% DV; fat 4.3g 7% DV; cholesterol 10mg 3% DV; sodium 996.4mg 40% DV.

Instant Pot Southern-Style Green Beans from a Can

prep: 10 mins cook: 30 mins additional: 5 mins total: 45 mins
Servings: 8
Ingredients

- 8 ounces thick cut bacon, cut into 1 inch pieces
- 1 cup diced yellow onion
- 2 tablespoons cider vinegar
- 4 (15 ounce) cans cut green beans, with liquid
- 2 teaspoons sea salt, or to taste
- ½ teaspoon black pepper
- 1 ½ pounds daikon (white radish), peeled and chopped

Directions
Step 1
Turn on a multi-functional pressure cooker (such as Instant Pot) and select Saute function. Add bacon and cook until almost crispy, about 8 minutes. Take your time cooking the bacon in order to render out all the fat. Add onions and cook, stirring frequently, until soft and translucent, about 3 minutes.
Step 2
Pour in vinegar and scrape up the brown bits from the bottom of the pot. Pour in beans and their liquid; season with salt and pepper. Stir in radishes. Close and lock the lid. Select high pressure according to manufacturer's instructions; set timer for 5 minutes. Allow 10 to 15 minutes for pressure to build.
Step 3
Release pressure carefully using the quick-release method according to manufacturer's instructions, about 5 minutes. Unlock and remove the lid.
Cook's Note:
Recipe Notes
If you want to make a smaller batch, scale down the ingredients but the cook time remains the same.
Nutrition Facts
Per Serving:
101.5 calories; protein 5g 10% DV; carbohydrates 11.3g 4% DV; fat 4.3g 7% DV; cholesterol 10mg 3% DV; sodium 996.4mg 40% DV.

Instant Pot Risotto

prep: 5 mins cook: 20 mins additional: 5 mins total: 30 mins
Servings: 3
Ingredients

- 1 cube chicken bouillon (such as Knorr)
- 2 cups hot water
- 2 tablespoons extra-virgin olive oil
- ¼ cup finely diced onion
- 1 clove garlic, minced
- 1 cup Arborio rice
- ¼ cup white wine
- 2 tablespoons butter

- ¼ cup grated Parmigiano-
  Reggiano cheese

- 2 teaspoons chopped fresh
  parsley

Directions
Step 1
Dissolve the chicken bouillon cube in the hot water and set aside.
Step 2
Turn on a multi-functional pressure cooker (such as Instant Pot) and select Saute function. Add olive oil to the pot. Add onion and cook for 1 minute. Add garlic and rice and stir until each grain of rice is coated with the oil mixture. Cook until rice is slightly toasted, about 2 minutes. Pour in white wine and simmer for about 30 seconds. Stir in chicken broth.
Step 3
Turn off Saute function. Close and lock the lid. Select high pressure according to manufacturer's instructions; set timer for 6 minutes. Allow 5 to 10 minutes for pressure to build.
Step 4
Release pressure carefully using the quick-release method according to manufacturer's instructions, about 5 minutes. Unlock and remove the lid. Add butter; stir until risotto is creamy, about 1 minute. Stir in Parmigiano-Reggiano cheese until melted and well combined. Serve sprinkled with parsley.
Nutrition Facts
Per Serving:
446.5 calories; protein 7.7g 15% DV; carbohydrates 57.2g 18% DV; fat 18.7g 29% DV; cholesterol 26.4mg 9% DV; sodium 547.4mg 22% DV.

Instant Pot Midwest Goulash

prep: 15 mins cook: 10 mins additional: 15 mins total: 40 mins
Servings: 4
Ingredients

- 1 tablespoon olive oil
- 1 pound ground turkey
- 2 small carrots, grated
- ½ onion, diced
- ½ green bell pepper, diced
- 1 tablespoon Italian seasoning, or to taste
- 1 teaspoon garlic powder, or to taste
- 1 teaspoon seasoned salt (such as Lawry's), or to taste

- 1 teaspoon ground black pepper, or to taste
- 1 ½ cups water
- 1 tablespoon Worcestershire sauce
- 1 ½ teaspoons beef bouillon granules
- 2 cups elbow macaroni
- 1 teaspoon paprika
- 1 (15 ounce) can petite diced tomatoes
- 1 (8 ounce) can tomato sauce

Directions
Step 1
Turn on a multi-functional pressure cooker (such as Instant Pot) and select Saute function. Add olive oil and turkey; cook until halfway browned and crumbly, 3 to

4 minutes. Add carrots, onion, bell pepper, Italian seasoning, garlic powder, seasoned salt, and black pepper.
Step 2
Mix water with Worcestershire sauce and bouillon granules in a small bowl. Pour into meat mixture and mix well. Bring to a simmer. Add macaroni and paprika and stir. Add tomatoes and tomato sauce, making sure not to stir after this addition. Close and lock the lid. Set timer for 4 minutes. Allow about 10 minutes for pressure to build.
Step 3
Release pressure carefully using the quick-release method according to manufacturer's instructions to prevent sauce from mixing with the steam, about 5 minutes. Unlock and remove the lid. Mix well.
Cook's Note:
You can also use Italian-seasoned diced tomatoes or stewed tomatoes instead of regular diced.
Nutrition Facts
Per Serving:
460.4 calories; protein 32.1g 64% DV; carbohydrates 53.1g 17% DV; fat 13.2g 20% DV; cholesterol 83.7mg 28% DV; sodium 1414.5mg 57% DV.

Instant Pot Beef Tips with Mushroom Gravy

prep: 10 mins cook: 50 mins additional: 15 mins total: 1 hr 15 mins
Servings: 4
Ingredients

- 1 pound beef sirloin tips
- 1 pinch salt and ground black pepper to taste
- 2 tablespoons all-purpose flour
- 1 tablespoon olive oil
- 1 small onion, chopped
- 6 medium (blank)s button mushrooms, sliced
- 1 cup beef broth
- ½ cup red wine
- 1 tablespoon Worcestershire sauce
- 1 (10.5 ounce) can condensed cream of mushroom soup

Directions
Step 1
Place beef tips in a bowl and season with salt and pepper. Add flour and stir to coat.
Step 2
Turn on a multi-functional pressure cooker (such as Instant Pot) and select Saute function. Add oil and let it get hot. Add beef tips and saute until browned, about 3 minutes; transfer to a bowl. Add onion and mushrooms and saute for 1 minute. Add broth, wine, and Worcestershire sauce; cook for 1 minute while scraping off the brown bits with a wooden spoon.
Step 3
Return beef tips to the pot and stir until everything is evenly combined. Pour condensed soup over top; do not stir.
Step 4

Close and lock the lid. Select high pressure according to manufacturer's instructions; set timer for 25 minutes. Allow 10 minutes for pressure to build.
Step 5
Release pressure carefully using the quick-release method according to manufacturer's instructions, about 5 minutes. Unlock and remove the lid. Let sit until gravy has thickened, about 10 minutes.

Cook's Note:
For a thicker gravy, mix 1/4 cup cold water with 2 tablespoons of cornstarch. Stir in the pot for the final 10 minutes of resting.
Nutrition Facts
Per Serving:
294.8 calories; protein 23g 46% DV; carbohydrates 12.1g 4% DV; fat 14.5g 22% DV; cholesterol 48.9mg 16% DV; sodium 802.7mg 32% DV.

Instant Pot Celery Soup

prep: 20 mins cook: 25 mins additional: 15 mins total: 1 hr
Servings: 4
Ingredients
- 2 tablespoons olive oil
- 2 pounds celery, sliced
- 1 large onion, sliced
- 3 cloves garlic, sliced
- ½ pound potatoes, peeled and chopped
- 4 cups vegetable broth
- ¼ teaspoon salt
- ⅛ teaspoon ground black pepper

Directions
Step 1
Combine olive oil, celery, onion, and garlic in a multi-functional pressure cooker (such as Instant Pot). Select Saute function and cook, stirring occasionally, for 5 minutes. Add potatoes, broth, salt, and pepper and stir. Close and lock the lid and set the steamer valve to Sealing.
Step 2
Select high pressure according to manufacturer's instructions; set timer for 10 minutes. Allow 10 to 15 minutes for pressure to build.
Step 3
Release pressure using the natural-release method according to manufacturer's instructions, about 15 minutes. Unlock and remove the lid.
Step 4
Use an electric hand mixer or blender to puree the soup until smooth. Serve while warm or let cool and serve as a chilled soup on a hot day.
Nutrition Facts
Per Serving:
188.2 calories; protein 4.3g 9% DV; carbohydrates 25.9g 8% DV; fat 7.7g 12% DV; cholesterolmg; sodium 792.4mg 32% DV.

Instant Pot Cabbage and Beef Soup

prep: 15 mins cook: 40 mins additional: 20 mins total: 1 hr 15 mins
Servings: 6
Ingredients

- 1 tablespoon olive oil
- 1 pound ground beef
- 1 teaspoon dried oregano
- 1 teaspoon dried thyme
- 1 cup chopped carrot
- 1 cup chopped Yukon Gold potato
- ½ onion, chopped
- 2 cloves garlic, chopped
- 8 cups water
- 1 (14.5 ounce) can Italian-style stewed tomatoes, drained and diced
- ½ head cabbage, cored and coarsely chopped
- 8 teaspoons vegetable bouillon base (such as Better Than Bouillon)
- 1 teaspoon salt, or to taste
- ½ teaspoon ground black pepper, or to taste

Directions
Step 1
Turn on a multi-functional pressure cooker (such as Instant Pot) and select Saute function for medium heat. When the display reads "Hot," add olive oil to coat the bottom of the pot. Add beef, oregano, and thyme; cook and stir until browned, breaking it apart as it cooks, 5 to 7 minutes. Add carrot, potato, onion, and garlic. Cook to soften, stirring frequently, about 5 minutes. Turn off Saute mode.

Step 2
Stir water, tomatoes with their juices, cabbage, vegetable base, salt, and pepper into the pot. Stir briefly together.

Step 3
Close and lock the lid. Select high pressure according to manufacturer's instructions; set timer for 20 minutes. Allow 10 to 15 minutes for pressure to build.

Step 4
Release pressure using the natural-release method according to manufacturer's instructions for 15 minutes. Release remaining pressure carefully using the quick-release method according to manufacturer's instructions, about 5 minutes. Unlock and remove the lid; stir. Serve while hot.

Nutrition Facts
Per Serving:
237.1 calories; protein 15.5g 31% DV; carbohydrates 18.5g 6% DV; fat 11.6g 18% DV; cholesterol 47.3mg 16% DV; sodium 626.9mg 25% DV.

Instant Pot Mongolian Chicken

prep: 10 mins cook: 20 mins additional: 15 mins total: 45 mins
Servings: 6
Ingredients
- 2 tablespoons olive oil
- 4 eaches boneless chicken breast, cut into cubes
- 1 cup chicken broth
- ½ cup brown sugar
- ½ cup soy sauce
- 1 carrot, chopped
- 4 eaches garlic cloves, minced
- 1 tablespoon minced fresh ginger root
- 1 teaspoon chili powder
- 2 tablespoons cornstarch
- ¼ cup water
- 1 teaspoon sesame seeds

Directions
Step 1
Turn on a multi-functional pressure cooker (such as Instant Pot) and select Saute function. Heat olive oil and add chicken cubes; cook until golden, stirring constantly, about 3 minutes. Stir in chicken broth, brown sugar, soy sauce, carrot, garlic, ginger, and chili powder. Close and lock the lid. Select high pressure according to manufacturer's instructions; set timer for 7 minutes. Allow 10 to 15 minutes for pressure to build.
Step 2
Release pressure using the natural-release method according to manufacturer's instructions, about 10 minutes. Complete releasing pressure carefully using the quick-release method according to manufacturer's instructions, about 5 minutes. Unlock and remove the lid. Reselect Saute function.
Step 3
Whisk cornstarch in 1/4 cup water until fully dissolved. Pour into the pot and stir to combine. Cook until sauce thickens, stirring gently, about 4 minutes. Sprinkle with sesame seeds before serving.
Nutrition Facts
Per Serving:
218.5 calories; protein 16.5g 33% DV; carbohydrates 23.4g 8% DV; fat 6.5g 10% DV; cholesterol 40mg 13% DV; sodium 1439.2mg 58% DV.

Pressure Cooker Messy Lasagna

prep: 10 mins cook: 10 mins total: 20 mins
Servings: 8
Ingredients
- 1 pound lean ground beef
- 1 onion, chopped
- 1 (16 ounce) package bow tie pasta (farfalle)
- 1 (15 ounce) can tomato sauce
- 1 (15 ounce) can stewed tomatoes
- 1 (10 ounce) package frozen spinach, thawed
- 1 clove garlic, minced
- 1 teaspoon oregano
- 1 teaspoon Italian seasoning
- 1 cup water to cover
- 1 (15 ounce) container ricotta cheese

- 1 cup shredded mozzarella cheese

Directions
Step 1
Heat pressure cooker over medium-high heat. Add ground beef and cook until browned, 3 to 5 minutes. Stir in onion; cook until translucent, 1 to 2 minutes. Stir in pasta, tomato sauce, stewed tomatoes, spinach, garlic, oregano, and Italian seasoning; mix well. Add water to cover.
Step 2
Cover pressure cooker and cook on high pressure according to manufacturer's instructions, about 5 minutes. Remove from heat and release pressure through quick-release method; open pressure cooker carefully.
Step 3
Stir ricotta cheese into pasta mixture; simmer until pasta is tender, 2 to 5 minutes more. Sprinkle mozzarella cheese over pasta mixture.
Cook's Notes:
Substitute sausage for the ground beef, if desired.
Substitute fresh spinach for the frozen, if desired.
Nutrition Facts
Per Serving:
468.2 calories; protein 29.3g 59% DV; carbohydrates 53g 17% DV; fat 15.5g 24% DV; cholesterol 59.8mg 20% DV; sodium 566.7mg 23% DV.

Instant Pot Cheesy Broccoli Rice

prep: 5 mins cook: 40 mins additional: 10 mins total: 55 mins
Servings: 4
Ingredients
- 1 tablespoon butter
- ¼ cup chopped onion
- 1 cup uncooked white rice
- 1 ½ cups chicken broth, divided
- 1 head broccoli, chopped
- ½ cup fat-free half-and-half
- 1 teaspoon garlic salt
- ½ teaspoon Italian seasoning
- ¼ teaspoon black pepper
- 1 cup shredded Cheddar cheese, divided

Directions
Step 1
Turn on a multi-functional pressure cooker (such as Instant Pot) and select Saute function. Add butter and stir until melted. Add onion and saute until golden brown, about 5 minutes. Stir in rice and pour in 1 1/4 cup chicken broth or as much as needed to cover rice. Close and lock the lid. Select rice setting according to manufacturer's instructions; set timer for 12 minutes. Allow 10 to 15 minutes for pressure to build.
Step 2
Release pressure carefully using the quick-release method according to manufacturer's instructions, about 5 minutes. Unlock and remove the lid. Add chopped broccoli and stir to combine. If rice looks dry, add remaining 1/4 cup chicken broth. Close lid and seal the vent. Select steam and set the timer for 5 minutes.

Step 3
Release pressure carefully using the quick-release method according to manufacturer's instructions, about 5 minutes. Pour in half-and-half, garlic salt, Italian seasoning, pepper, and 3/4 cup Cheddar cheese. Stir to combine.
Step 4
Set an oven rack about 6 inches from the heat source and preheat the oven's broiler. Grease an 8-inch square casserole dish.
Step 5
Transfer broccoli mixture to the prepared casserole dish and top with remaining Cheddar cheese. Broil until cheese is golden brown, about 5 minutes.
Nutrition Facts
Per Serving:
370.8 calories; protein 13.8g 28% DV; carbohydrates 48.5g 16% DV; fat 13.5g 21% DV; cholesterol 41.1mg 14% DV; sodium 1155.1mg 46% DV.

Gluten-Free Northern Italian Autumn Minestrone

prep: 30 mins cook: 40 mins additional: 8 hrs 10 mins total: 9 hrs 20 mins
Servings: 8
Ingredients

- 1 cup dried cranberry beans
- 1 medium carrot
- 1 small yellow onion
- 1 stalk celery
- ½ small red bell pepper
- ¼ cup olive oil
- 15 ounces potatoes, peeled and diced
- 12 ounces diced carrots
- 12 ounces zucchini, diced
- 10 ounces fresh pumpkin, diced
- 4 ounces diced yellow onion
- 2 tablespoons chopped fresh oregano
- 1 tablespoon minced fresh rosemary
- 1 bay leaf
- 8 cups vegetable broth, divided
- 1 tablespoon salt
- 6 ounces gluten-free elbow pasta
- 1 fresh hot pepper, minced
- 6 tablespoons finely grated Parmigiano-Reggiano cheese

Directions
Step 1
Place cranberry beans into a large container and cover with several inches of cool water; let soak, 8 hours to overnight. Drain.
Step 2
Shred carrot, yellow onion, celery, and red pepper in a food processor to create a sofrito mixture.
Step 3
Heat oil in a 7-quart pressure cooker over medium-high heat. Add sofrito mixture and saute until softened, 3 to 5 minutes. Add soaked beans, potatoes, diced carrots, zucchini, pumpkin, and diced onion. Cook and stir until warmed through, 3 to 5 minutes more. Add oregano, rosemary, and bay leaf. Stir well to coat vegetables with oil and seasonings.

Step 4
Add enough broth to cover vegetables by 1 inch. Close the pressure cooker lid and bring up to pressure, about 10 minutes. Cook an additional 10 minutes from the first whistle.
Step 5
Allow pressure to release naturally and remove lid, about 10 minutes. Taste and adjust salt if necessary. Add additional broth to allow for cooking the pasta. Bring to a boil and add pasta. Cook, stirring occasionally, until tender but still firm to the bite, about 8 minutes. Add more boiling broth if needed during cooking.
Step 6
Ladle soup into bowls and top with minced hot pepper and Parmigiano-Reggiano cheese.
Cook's Notes:
If you can get fresh cranberry beans, you may skip the soaking time. Use 3 cups fresh beans in place of the 1 cup dried.
Cranberry beans also called borlotti beans can be substituted with pinto beans.

Nutrition Facts
Per Serving:
355.6 calories; protein 12.5g 25% DV; carbohydrates 57.6g 19% DV; fat 9.4g 14% DV; cholesterol 3.3mg 1% DV; sodium 1438.6mg 58% DV.

Chocolate Mousse Cheesecake

prep: 15 mins cook: 1 hr additional: 1 day total: 1 day
Servings: 10
Ingredients

- ½ cup chocolate cookie crumbs
- 1 pinch ground cinnamon
- 8 (1 ounce) squares semisweet chocolate
- 1 tablespoon butter
- 2 (8 ounce) packages cream cheese, softened
- 1 cup heavy whipping cream
- 1 teaspoon vanilla extract
- ⅔ cup white sugar
- 2 large eggs eggs, beaten
- 1 ½ tablespoons unsweetened cocoa powder
- 1 ½ cups water

Directions
Step 1
Grease an 8-inch springform pan that will fit inside the pressure cooker. Mix the chocolate wafer crumbs and cinnamon together. Sprinkle the crumb mixture on the bottom of springform pan, pressing gently to form the crust.
Step 2
Melt chocolate and butter together and set aside.
Step 3
With a food processor or electric mixer, process cream cheese until smooth. Add chocolate mixture, and process until mixture is well-mixed and uniformly colored. Pour in the cream, vanilla extract, sugar, and eggs. Beat well. Sieve cocoa powder over batter, and pulse or mix on low speed until cocoa is thoroughly incorporated. Pour mixture over crumbs in pan. Cover cake with a piece of waxed paper. Wrap the entire pan with aluminum foil.

Step 4
Add water to pressure cooker. Place pan on the trivet in pressure cooker. Seal **the** cooker and bring it up to 15 pounds (high) pressure. Reduce the heat to maintain the pressure, and cook 45 to 50 minutes. Remove cooker from heat, and let the pressure drop on its own. Remove cheesecake from cooker, and let cool to room temperature in pan on a wire rack.
Step 5
Remove cheesecake from pan, and refrigerate for 8 hours before serving.
Nutrition Facts
Per Serving:
454.1 calories; protein 7.3g 15% DV; carbohydrates 32.7g 11% DV; fat 34.7g 53% DV; cholesterol 122.3mg 41% DV; sodium 196.5mg 8% DV.

Beef Stroganoff in an Instant

prep: 15 mins cook: 50 mins additional: 10 mins total: 1 hr 15 mins
Servings: 8
Ingredients

- 1 tablespoon extra-virgin olive oil
- 1 medium red onion, chopped
- 2 ½ tablespoons Worcestershire sauce
- 3 cloves garlic, diced
- 1 teaspoon beef base (such as Better Than Bouillon)
- 1 tablespoon ground black pepper, or to taste
- 1 teaspoon dried thyme
- 1 teaspoon salt
- ¾ cup dry vermouth, divided
- 2 pounds New York strip steaks, cut into thin pieces
- 3 cups sliced mushrooms
- 2 cups beef broth, divided
- 1 (16 ounce) package wide egg noodles
- 2 tablespoons all-purpose flour
- ¾ cup sour cream

Directions
Step 1
Turn on a multi-functional pressure cooker (such as Instant Pot) and select Saute function. Heat oil in the pot. Saute onion until barely tender, about 3 minutes. Mix in Worcestershire sauce, garlic, beef base, pepper, thyme, and salt.
Step 2
Pour in 1/4 cup vermouth; deglaze the pot by scraping the bottom with a wooden spoon. Add steaks; saute until browned, about 6 minutes. Turn off Saute mode. Add remaining vermouth, mushrooms, and 1 1/2 cups beef broth. Mix together gently.
Step 3
Close and lock the lid. Select high pressure according to manufacturer's instructions; set timer for 10 minutes. Allow 10 to 15 minutes for pressure to build.
Step 4
Release pressure carefully using the quick-release method according to manufacturer's instructions, about 5 minutes. Unlock and remove the lid. Stir in noodles. Lock the lid and cook on high pressure until noodles are tender, about 3 minutes. Allow 5 to 10 minutes for pressure to build.
Step 5

Pour remaining 1/2 cup beef broth into a microwave-safe bowl. Microwave until hot, about 1 minute. Dissolve flour in the broth.
Step 6
Release pressure carefully using the quick-release method according to manufacturer's instructions, about 5 minutes. Open lid and stir in the beef broth mixture. Let thicken, 3 to 5 minutes. Stir again. Add sour cream; stir until completely combined.
Cook's Notes:
Yellow onion can be substituted for the red onion.
Use any steak you have available.
Flour can be substituted for the cornstarch.
Nutrition Facts
Per Serving:
521.3 calories; protein 28.5g 57% DV; carbohydrates 49.7g 16% DV; fat 20.3g 31% DV; cholesterol 115.6mg 39% DV; sodium 659.2mg 26% DV.

Instant Pot Coconut Rice

prep: 5 mins cook: 15 mins additional: 1 hr 10 mins total: 1 hr 30 mins
Servings: 8
Ingredients

- 2 cups uncooked short-grain white rice
- 1 (14 ounce) can unsweetened coconut milk
- 1 cup chicken stock
- 2 tablespoons white sugar
- 1 teaspoon fine sea salt

Directions
Step 1
Rinse rice under cold tap water until water runs clear. Soak rice in a bowl of water for 1 hour.
Step 2
Combine coconut milk, chicken stock, sugar, and salt in a multi-functional pressure cooker (such as Instant Pot).
Step 3
Drain rice and stir into the pressure cooker. Close and lock the lid. Select high pressure according to manufacturer's instructions; set timer for 5 minutes. Allow 10 to 15 minutes for pressure to build.
Step 4
Release pressure using the natural-release method according to manufacturer's instructions, about 10 minutes. Unlock lid and open carefully; fluff rice with a fork.
Cook's Notes:
Soaking the rice is optional but optimal.
Use homemade chicken stock if possible. Substitute with coconut water for a vegan version.
Nutrition Facts
Per Serving:
289 calories; protein 4.3g 9% DV; carbohydrates 44.2g 14% DV; fat 10.8g 17% DV; cholesterol 0.1mg; sodium 312.6mg 13% DV.

Sausage, Kale, and White Bean Soup

prep: 15 mins cook: 1 hr additional: 8 hrs total: 9 hrs 15 mins
Servings: 8
Ingredients

- 1 cup dry navy beans
- 1 large bunch kale, rinsed, stemmed and chopped
- 1 tablespoon olive oil
- 1 pound spicy linguica sausage, sliced
- 1 cup chopped shallots
- 4 cups chicken broth
- 1 pinch salt and pepper to taste
- ½ teaspoon hot sauce, or to taste

Directions
Step 1
Place the navy beans into a large container and cover with several inches of cool water; let stand 8 hours or overnight. Drain and rinse before using.
Step 2
Cook the soaked beans in a pressure cooker in 4 cups of water for 25 minutes. Use the natural release method to release pressure. Do not drain.
Step 3
Bring a separate pot of salted water to a boil. Add the kale and simmer until kale is bright green and tender, about 2 minutes. Drain in a strainer, and cool under cold running water. Set aside.
Step 4
Heat olive oil over medium heat in the soup pot. Brown the linguica slices on each side, about 5 minutes. Remove from the pot with a slotted spoon and set aside. Add shallots to pot and cook until soft, about 3 minutes. Pour in a splash of chicken broth and scrape up any browned bits of sausage.
Step 5
Return the sausage to the pot along with the beans and their cooking liquid. Stir in the chicken broth. Bring soup to a boil, reduce heat to low, and simmer uncovered for 15 minutes. Add the kale and cook about 4 minutes longer. Season with salt, pepper, and hot sauce to taste.
Nutrition Facts
Per Serving:
372.8 calories; protein 19.2g 38% DV; carbohydrates 20.3g 7% DV; fat 23.8g 37% DV; cholesterol 49.9mg 17% DV; sodium 726.5mg 29% DV.

Instant Pot Roasted Garlic

prep: 5 mins cook: 20 mins additional: 15 mins total: 40 mins
Servings: 4
Ingredients
- 1 cup water, or as needed
- 1 bulb garlic
- 1 tablespoon olive oil, or as needed
- 1 pinch salt

Directions
Step 1
Place the steamer basket in the bottom of a multi-functional pressure cooker (such as Instant Pot). Add water up to the bottom of the steamer basket.
Step 2
Cut 1/4 inch off the top of the garlic bulb and place into the steamer basket. Drizzle with olive oil and sprinkle with salt. Close and lock the lid. Select Poultry function according to manufacturer's instructions; set timer for 10 minutes. Allow 10 to 15 minutes for pressure to build.
Step 3
Release pressure using the natural-release method according to manufacturer's instructions, about 10 minutes. Unlock and remove the lid. Remove garlic and cool until easily handled, about 5 minutes. Squeeze garlic pulp into a glass jar and refrigerate.
Cook's Note:
Double or triple the recipe if desired. You can cook as many garlic bulbs as will fit in the basket.
Nutrition Facts
Per Serving:
51.2 calories; protein 0.9g 2% DV; carbohydrates 4.6g 2% DV; fat 3.4g 5% DV; cholesterolmg; sodium 42.9mg 2% DV.

Quick Short Rib Stew

prep: 20 mins cook: 45 mins total: 1 hr 5 mins
Servings: 6
Ingredients

- ½ cup all-purpose flour for coating
- 4 pounds beef short ribs
- 2 tablespoons canola or vegetable oil
- 1 cup hot water
- 2 cubes beef bouillon
- 1 (28 ounce) can diced or stewed tomatoes
- 2 cloves garlic, thinly sliced
- 2 medium onions, chopped
- 6 medium carrots, peeled and sliced
- 6 medium potatoes, peeled and cubed
- 3 tablespoons all-purpose flour, dissolved in
- 1 cup water
- 1 (15 ounce) can peas, with liquid
- ½ teaspoon Salt and pepper to taste

Directions
Step 1
Heat a large skillet over medium-high heat. Place 1/2 cup of flour in a heavy plastic bag or large bowl; add the ribs and toss until completely coated. Pour the oil into the preheated pan, heat until shimmering. Shake any excess flour off of the ribs, then add them to the hot oil. Brown well on all sides without burning, about 10 minutes.
Step 2
While the ribs are browning, stir together the hot water and bouillon cubes in a pressure cooker until dissolved. Using tongs, remove the ribs from the skillet, and

place into the pressure cooker. Seal according to manufacturer's directions and cook for 25 minutes.
Step 3
After 25 minutes, release pressure, and open cooker according to manufacturer's directions. Pour in the canned tomatoes, garlic, onion, and carrots. Simmer, uncovered until the vegetables are tender, about 20 minutes. Meanwhile, cook the diced potatoes in enough water to cover until tender, about 20 minutes.
Step 4
Remove the meat to a serving platter. Stir together 3 tablespoons of flour with 1 cup of water. Stir into the vegetables, and cook until the sauce thickens, about 5 minutes.
Step 5
Drain the cooked potatoes, and add to the stew along with the can of peas. Heat until warmed through, then season to taste with salt and pepper.

Nutrition Facts
Per Serving:
987.6 calories; protein 37.9g 76% DV; carbohydrates 70g 23% DV; fat 61g 94% DV; cholesterol 124.4mg 42% DV; sodium 938.2mg 38% DV.

Instant Pot Beef and Vegetable Soup

prep: 30 mins cook: 50 mins additional: 10 mins total: 1 hr 30 mins
Servings: 8
Ingredients
- 1 tablespoon olive oil
- 2 pounds boneless beef chuck roast, cut into cubes, or to taste
- 5 large carrots, chopped
- 1 large yellow onion, chopped
- 2 stalks celery, chopped
- 6 cups water
- 3 large turnips, peeled and diced
- 1 pound fresh green beans, trimmed and sliced
- 2 tablespoons tomato paste
- 2 tablespoons salt, or more to taste
- 2 tablespoons garlic powder, or more to taste
- 1 tablespoon onion powder, or more to taste
- 1 tablespoon celery seed
- 2 leaf (blank)s bay leaves
- 1 pinch ground black pepper to taste

Directions
Step 1
Heat olive oil in a multi-functional pressure cooker (such as Instant Pot) and select Saute function. Cook beef cubes until brown on all sides, 5 to 10 minutes. Transfer to a plate. Cook carrots, onion, and celery until translucent, about 5 minutes. Return beef to the pot; add water, turnips, green beans, tomato paste, salt, garlic powder, onion powder, celery seed, and bay leaves.
Step 2
Close and lock the lid. Select high pressure according to manufacturer's instructions; set timer for 30 minutes. Allow 10 to 15 minutes for pressure to build.
Step 3

Release pressure using the natural-release method according to manufacturer's instructions, 10 to 40 minutes. Unlock and remove the lid. Taste the soup; add more salt, garlic, onion, and pepper, if needed.
Cook's Note:
Sometimes we mix 1 tablespoon xanthan gum with some water to thicken it up.
Nutrition Facts
Per Serving:
264.8 calories; protein 16.4g 33% DV; carbohydrates 18.2g 6% DV; fat 14.7g 23% DV; cholesterol 51.5mg 17% DV; sodium 1905.2mg 76% DV.

Instant Pot Turkey Cheeseburger Soup

prep: 20 mins cook: 35 mins additional: 5 mins total: 1 hr
Servings: 8
Ingredients

- 1 pound ground turkey
- 2 teaspoons seasoned salt (such as LAWRY'S)
- 1 tablespoon butter
- 2 medium (blank)s carrots, diced
- 2 stalks celery, diced
- 1 medium onion, diced
- 2 tablespoons all-purpose flour
- 1 teaspoon dried dill weed
- ½ teaspoon ground black pepper
- 3 ½ cups beef broth
- 2 medium (blank)s Yukon gold potatoes, diced
- ¼ head cauliflower
- 1 (8 ounce) package shredded sharp Cheddar cheese

Directions
Step 1
Turn on a multi-functional pressure cooker (such as Instant Pot) and select Saute function. Add turkey and seasoned salt; saute until browned, about 5 minutes. Remove turkey.
Step 2
Melt butter in the pot. Add carrots, celery, and onion; cook until just starting to soften, about 5 minutes. Add flour, dill, and pepper; cook for about 1 minute. Return turkey to the pot; add broth and potatoes. Top with cauliflower. Close and lock the lid.
Step 3
Select high pressure according to manufacturer's instructions; set timer for 10 minutes. Allow 10 to 15 minutes for pressure to build.
Step 4
Release pressure carefully using the quick-release method according to manufacturer's instructions, about 5 minutes. Unlock and remove the lid.
Step 5
Remove the cauliflower and 1 cup of the soup liquid; blend together until smooth and creamy. Add Cheddar cheese and season to tate. Stir cauliflower puree into the pot with the rest of the soup until cheese is completely melted.
Cook's Note:
Leave cauliflower whole or in big chunks for easy removal.
Nutrition Facts
Per Serving:

267.1 calories; protein 21g 42% DV; carbohydrates 11.8g 4% DV; fat 15.4g 24% DV; cholesterol 75mg 25% DV; sodium 817.3mg 33% DV

Instant Pot Chicken Alfredo

prep: 5 mins cook: 30 mins additional: 15 mins total: 50 mins
Servings: 3
Ingredients
- 1 (6 ounce) skinless, boneless chicken breast
- 2 tablespoons butter, divided
- 1 ½ teaspoons garlic salt, divided
- 1 teaspoon cantanzaro herbs (from Savory Spice Shop)
- 1 clove garlic, minced
- 2 cups penne pasta
- 16 ounces heavy whipping cream
- 2 ½ cups freshly grated Parmesan cheese
- 1 pinch freshly ground black pepper to taste

Directions
Step 1
Slice chicken breast into 3 thin filets. Sprinkle all sides with 1 teaspoon garlic salt and cantanzaro herbs.
Step 2
Turn on a multi-functional pressure cooker (such as Instant Pot) and select Saute function. Melt 1 tablespoon butter. Add chicken breasts and sear on both sides until golden brown, about 5 minutes. Remove and set aside.
Step 3
Wipe out the pot. Melt remaining 1 tablespoon butter, and cook garlic until fragrant, about 1 minute. Add pasta and stir to coat in butter. Pour in cream and stir to thoroughly combine with pasta.
Step 4
Place an elevated steamer rack inside the Instant Pot. Wrap chicken breasts in parchment paper and place on top of the steamer rack.
Step 5
Close and lock the lid. Select high pressure according to manufacturer's instructions; set timer for 10 minutes. Allow 10 to 15 minutes for pressure to build.
Step 6
Release pressure using the natural-release method according to manufacturer's instructions for 10 minutes. Release remaining pressure carefully using the quick-release method according to manufacturer's instructions, about 5 minutes. Unlock and remove the lid. Remove rack with chicken. Stir remaining garlic salt and Parmesan cheese into sauce.
Step 7
Divide pasta into 3 serving bowls and top each with 1 chicken breast filet. Top with additional Parmesan and freshly ground black pepper if desired.
Nutrition Facts
Per Serving:
1117.7 calories; protein 47.2g 94% DV; carbohydrates 43g 14% DV; fat 85.3g 131% DV; cholesterol 318.8mg 106% DV; sodium 2068.5mg 83% DV

Instant Pot Roasted Melting Sweet Potatoes

prep: 5 mins cook: 20 mins additional: 5 mins total: 30 mins
Servings: 2
Ingredients

- ½ cup butter
- 1 pound sweet potatoes, peeled and cut into 1-inch slices
- ¾ cup vegetable broth

- 1 teaspoon ground thyme
- 1 teaspoon salt
- ½ teaspoon ground black pepper

Directions
Step 1
Turn on a multi-functional pressure cooker (such as Instant Pot) and select Saute function. Melt butter. Add sweet potato rounds in a single layer and cook until golden, about 4 minutes. Flip and cook for 4 minutes more. Pour vegetable broth over the sweet potatoes and sprinkle with thyme, salt, and pepper.
Step 2
Close and lock lid. Select high pressure according to manufacturer's instructions; set timer for 2 minutes. Allow 10 to 15 minutes for pressure to build.
Step 3
Release pressure carefully using the quick-release method according to manufacturer's instructions, about 5 minutes. Unlock and remove lid.
Nutrition Facts
Per Serving:
616.7 calories; protein 4.5g 9% DV; carbohydrates 48.4g 16% DV; fat 46.4g 71% DV; cholesterol 122mg 41% DV; sodium 1787.6mg 72% DV.

Instant Pot Asparagus Risotto

prep: 10 mins cook: 30 mins additional: 10 mins total: 50 mins
Servings: 4
Ingredients

- 3 tablespoons unsalted butter
- 2 eaches shallots, finely chopped
- 2 cloves garlic, minced
- 1 pound asparagus spears, trimmed and cut into 1-inch pieces
- ½ cup dry white wine
- 1 ½ cups Arborio rice
- 3 ½ cups chicken broth

- ½ cup heavy cream
- ½ teaspoon salt
- ¼ teaspoon ground black pepper
- ¼ teaspoon dried thyme
- ½ cup shredded Parmesan cheese
- 2 tablespoons lemon juice

Directions
Step 1
Turn on a multi-functional pressure cooker (such as Instant Pot) and select Saute function. Add butter and melt. Stir in shallots and garlic; cook for 2 minutes.

Remove shallots and garlic with a slotted spoon and set aside. Add asparagus and saute in butter for 2 minutes; remove and set aside on a plate.
Step 2
Return shallots and garlic to the Instant Pot and pour in wine. Stir well, scraping the bottom of the pot with a wooden or plastic spoon, for 30 seconds. Stir in rice and saute in the wine mixture for 2 1/2 minutes, stirring constantly and scraping the bottom of the pot to loosen any brown bits. Stir in chicken broth, cream, salt, pepper, and thyme. Cancel Saute function.
Step 3
Close and lock the lid. Select high pressure according to manufacturer's instructions; set timer for 6 minutes. Allow 10 to 15 minutes for pressure to build.
Step 4
Release pressure carefully using the quick-release method according to manufacturer's instructions, about 5 minutes. Unlock and remove the lid. Gradually stir in Parmesan cheese and lemon juice, stirring until cheese is melted. Stir in reserved asparagus pieces. Allow risotto to thicken in the pot, uncovered, for 3 to 4 minutes before serving.
Nutrition Facts
Per Serving:
611.4 calories; protein 14.5g 29% DV; carbohydrates 81.3g 26% DV; fat 23.1g 36% DV; cholesterol 76.2mg 25% DV; sodium 1498.2mg 60% DV.

Instant Pot Creamy Vanilla Rice Pudding

prep: 5 mins cook: 30 mins additional: 10 mins total: 45 mins
Servings: 8
Ingredients
- 3 cups cooked short-grain rice
- 2 ¼ cups milk, divided
- ½ cup white sugar
- ¼ teaspoon salt
- 2 eaches egg yolks, whisked well
- ¼ cup heavy cream
- 1 teaspoon vanilla extract
- 1 pinch ground cinnamon, or as needed

Directions
Step 1
Combine cooked rice, 2 cups milk, sugar, and salt in a multi-functional pressure cooker (such as Instant Pot) and stir well. Close and lock the lid. Select porridge function according to manufacturer's instructions and seal the vent. Set timer for 20 minutes. Allow 10 to 15 minutes for pressure to build.
Step 2
Release pressure using the natural-release method according to manufacturer's instructions, 10 to 40 minutes. Unlock and carefully remove the lid.
Step 3
Whisk egg yolks together well in a bowl. Add a small amount of cooked porridge and whisk quickly into yolks. Pour mixture into the pot and stir to combine well with rice. Add heavy cream, remaining milk, and vanilla extract. Stir to combine completely.
Step 4
Serve rice pudding in individual bowls garnished with cinnamon.
Nutrition Facts

Per Serving:
214 calories; protein 4.7g 10% DV; carbohydrates 36.3g 12% DV; fat 5.3g 8% DV; cholesterol 66.9mg 22% DV; sodium 105.7mg 4% DV.

Boneless Turkey Breast in the Instant Pot

prep: 25 mins cook: 55 mins total: 1 hr 20 mins
Servings: 8
Ingredients

- 1 tablespoon ground paprika
- 1 tablespoon herbes de Provence
- 1 teaspoon seasoned salt
- 1 pinch salt and ground black pepper to taste
- 1 (3 pound) frozen boneless turkey breast in mesh, thawed, with gravy packet reserved
- 2 tablespoons extra-virgin olive oil, divided
- 1 ½ cups chicken stock
- 3 stalks celery, cut into 4-inch pieces
- ½ onion, cut into 1/2-inch slices
- ½ cup water, or as needed
- 2 tablespoons unsalted butter
- 2 tablespoons all-purpose flour

Directions
Step 1
Combine paprika, herbes de Provence, seasoned salt, salt, and pepper in a small bowl. Place the trivet of a multi-functional pressure cooker (such as Instant Pot) on a work surface.
Step 2
Pat all sides of thawed turkey breast with paper towels until dry. Be sure to leave the mesh in place, as this holds the turkey together. Rub turkey with about 2 teaspoons olive oil, then rub with dry seasonings. Set gravy packet aside for later use.
Step 3
Turn on the cooker and select Saute function. Allow the inner pot to heat, 1 to 2 minutes. Add remaining oil to the hot pot, then add turkey breast and brown on all sides, about 5 minutes. Carefully remove turkey breast and set on the trivet. Pour chicken stock into the hot pot and scrape up any browned bits with a wooden spoon. Place the trivet and turkey breast into the pot and place celery and onions around it. Cancel Saute function.
Step 4
Close and lock the lid, set the valve to seal, and select high pressure according to manufacturer's instructions. Set timer for 25 minutes. Allow 10 to 15 minutes for pressure to build.
Step 5
Release pressure using the natural-release method according to manufacturer's instructions, about 15 minutes. Release any remaining pressure carefully using the quick-release method according to manufacturer's instructions.
Step 6
Open the pot and check internal temperature of the turkey with an instant-read thermometer. Safe internal temperature is at least 165 degrees F (74 degrees C). Lift turkey out of the pot and place on a cutting board; cover with aluminum foil. Remove the trivet and turn off the cooker.

Step 7
Strain cooking liquid into a glass measuring cup. Add enough water to make 1 1/2 cups liquid.
Step 8
Return the inner pot to the cooker, add butter, and select Saute function. Sprinkle flour into the melted butter and whisk briskly to avoid lumps. Whisk bubbling mixture for about 2 minutes, then gradually add the cooking liquid, stirring constantly. Pour in the contents of the gravy packet; cook and stir until mixture comes to a boil and thickens slightly, 5 to 10 minutes. Cancel Saute function and pour gravy into a serving container.
Step 9
Slice turkey and serve warm with gravy.
Cook's Note:
Turkey stock can be used in place of chicken stock.
Nutrition Facts
Per Serving:
352.9 calories; protein 43.2g 86% DV; carbohydrates 3.4g 1% DV; fat 17.5g 27% DV; cholesterol 117.3mg 39% DV; sodium 369.3mg 15% DV.

Instant Pot Bison Pasta (Pasta Bisonte)

prep: 15 mins cook: 21 mins additional: 5 mins total: 41 mins
Servings: 6
Ingredients

- 12 ounces ground bison
- 1 ½ cups diced onion
- 1 ½ cups diced red bell pepper
- 2 tablespoons olive oil
- 1 (8 ounce) package sliced baby portobello mushrooms
- ½ cup chopped fresh basil
- 4 cloves garlic, chopped
- 1 tablespoon dried oregano
- 1 bay leaf
- 2 (14.5 ounce) cans diced tomatoes
- 1 cup water
- ½ cup red wine
- 1 tablespoon tomato paste
- 1 (16 ounce) package trottole pasta
- ½ teaspoon salt
- ½ teaspoon onion powder
- ½ teaspoon garlic powder

Directions
Step 1
Turn on a multi-functional pressure cooker (such as Instant Pot) and select Saute function; heat until indicator reads 'Hot.' Add bison, onion, red bell pepper, and olive oil. Saute until bison is browned and crumbly, 5 to 7 minutes. Add mushrooms; saute until slightly softened, 1 to 2 minutes.
Step 2
Stir basil, garlic, oregano, and bay leaf into the bison mixture. Add tomatoes, water, wine, and tomato paste. Turn cooker off. Add pasta; stir until coated. Mix in salt, onion powder, and garlic powder.
Step 3

Set cooker to Manual. Close and lock the lid. Select high pressure according to manufacturer's instructions; set timer for 5 minutes. Allow 10 to 15 minutes for pressure to build.
Step 4
Release pressure carefully using the quick-release method according to manufacturer's instructions, about 5 minutes. Unlock and remove lid. Stir well.
Cook's Notes:
Use roasted garlic powder if available.
Use any kind of bell peppers you prefer.
You can replace the oregano with Italian herb mix.
Any variety of pasta works in this recipe. I used Italian trottole pasta, which is a bit thicker and takes a little longer to cook normally. Reduce cooking time to 4 minutes for more delicate pasta like farfalle. If it is too al dente for your taste, place the lid on and let it stand for another minute or two until it reaches your desired firmness.
Nutrition Facts
Per Serving:
459 calories; protein 23.2g 46% DV; carbohydrates 70.7g 23% DV; fat 6.8g 11% DV; cholesterol 29mg 10% DV; sodium 460.5mg 18% DV.

Instant Pot Chicken Drumsticks

prep: 20 mins cook: 25 mins additional: 8 hrs 20 mins total: 9 hrs 5 mins
Servings: 6
Ingredients

- 1 ½ cups orange juice
- 1 lime, juiced
- 1 lemon, juiced
- 1 tablespoon chili powder
- 2 cloves garlic, crushed
- 1 teaspoon ground cumin
- 1 teaspoon dried oregano
- 1 teaspoon garlic salt
- ½ teaspoon ground chipotle powder
- 6 eaches chicken drumsticks
- ½ onion, sliced and separated into rings
- 2 tablespoons chopped fresh cilantro

Directions
Step 1
Combine orange juice, lime juice, lemon juice, chili powder, garlic, cumin, oregano, garlic salt, and chipotle powder in a bowl. Pour into a resealable plastic bag and add chicken drumsticks, onion, and cilantro. Seal the bag and refrigerate for at least 8 hours to overnight, turning the bag frequently.
Step 2
Pour marinade into a multi-functional pressure cooker (such as Instant Pot). Place the rack inside the pot and place drumsticks on top. Close and lock the lid. Select high pressure according to manufacturer's instructions; set timer for 15 minutes. Allow 10 to 15 minutes for pressure to build.
Step 3
Release pressure using the natural-release method for 15 minutes. Release remaining pressure using the quick-release method according to manufacturer's instructions, about 5 minutes. Unlock and remove the lid.

Cook's Note:
If crispy chicken is desired, place drumsticks under a broiler and cook for 4 minutes, turning after 2 minutes.
Nutrition Facts
Per Serving:
239.3 calories; protein 16.7g 34% DV; carbohydrates 18.7g 6% DV; fat 11.6g 18% DV; cholesterol 60.5mg 20% DV; sodium 507.7mg 20% DV.

Instant Pot Butternut Squash and Pear Soup

prep: 10 mins cook: 40 mins additional: 10 mins total: 1 hr
Servings: 6
Ingredients

- 1 (3 pound) butternut squash
- 1 cup water
- 1 tablespoon olive oil
- ½ medium onion, quartered
- 2 cloves garlic, peeled
- 2 eaches ripe pears - peeled, cored, and chopped into 1-inch chunks
- 1 ½ teaspoons salt
- ¾ teaspoon ground sage
- 4 cups chicken broth
- ½ cup heavy cream

Directions
Step 1
Cut butternut squash into 4 pieces and remove seeds. Pour water into the bottom of a multi-functional electric pressure cooker and place trivet inside. Place squash on trivet, close lid, and set seal valve. Select high pressure according to manufacturer's instructions; set timer for 10 minutes. Allow 10 to 15 minutes for pressure to build.
Step 2
Release pressure carefully using the quick-release method according to manufacturer's instructions, about 5 minutes. Unlock and remove the lid. Drain out the water and wipe the bottom of the pot dry. Remove squash skin and discard. Roughly chop any large pieces into smaller 1- to 2-inch chunks. Set aside.
Step 3
Select the Saute function and heat olive oil. Saute onion and garlic for 1 to 2 minutes. Add pears, salt, and sage; cook for 1 to 2 minutes more. Turn pressure cooker off. Add the squash and chicken broth. Close lid and seal valve. Select high pressure; set timer for 5 minutes. Allow 10 to 15 minutes for pressure to build.
Step 4
Release pressure manually and remove lid. Blend soup until smooth using an immersion blender. Stir in heavy cream.
Cook's Notes:
Use vegetable broth to make it vegetarian.
If you do not have an immersion blender, blend soup in batches in a blender.
Nutrition Facts
Per Serving:
240.1 calories; protein 3.9g 8% DV; carbohydrates 37.7g 12% DV; fat 10.3g 16% DV; cholesterol 31.2mg 10% DV; sodium 1376.1mg 55% DV.

Pressure Cooker Italian Chicken Soup

prep: 25 mins cook: 25 mins total: 50 mins
Servings: 8
Ingredients

-
- 2 teaspoons olive oil
- 4 eaches Italian turkey sausage links, casings removed
- 1 medium onion, diced
- 3 cloves garlic, minced
- ½ cup pearl barley
- 1 cup green lentils
- 1 bone-in chicken breast half, skin removed
- ½ cup chopped fresh parsley
- 3 cups chicken stock
- 1 (15 ounce) can chickpeas (garbanzo beans), drained
- 1 (16 ounce) bag fresh spinach leaves, chopped
- 1 cup mild salsa

Directions
Step 1
heat 1 teaspoon olive oil in a pressure cooker over medium heat. Add sausage meat, and cook until browned, breaking it into crumbles. Remove sausage to a plate and drain oil. Add another 1 teaspoon of olive oil to pressure cooker; cook onion and garlic until onion is transparent. Add barley and stir 1 minute. Return sausage to pressure cooker. Add lentils, chicken, parsley, and chicken stock to cooker, adding enough stock to completely cover chicken. Close cover securely; place pressure regulator on vent pipe. Bring pressure cooker to full pressure over high heat (this may take 15 minutes). Reduce heat to medium high; cook for 9 minutes. Pressure regulator should maintain a slow steady rocking motion; adjust heat if necessary.

Step 2
Remove pressure cooker from heat; use quick-release following manufacturer's instructions or allow pressure to drop on its own. Open cooker and remove chicken; shred meat and return to soup. Add garbanzo beans, spinach and salsa; stir to blend and heat through before serving.

Nutrition Facts
Per Serving:
244.7 calories; protein 17.4g 35% DV; carbohydrates 37.3g 12% DV; fat 3.3g 5% DV; cholesterol 16.2mg 5% DV; sodium 527.1mg 21% DV.

Pork Chops with Oniony Mashed Potatoes and Cider Gravy

prep: 15 mins cook: 36 mins additional: 5 mins total: 56 mins
Servings: 2
Ingredients

- 2 (1-inch thick) bone-in center-cut pork chops
- 1 teaspoon sea salt
- ½ teaspoon dried thyme
- ½ teaspoon dried rosemary
- ¼ teaspoon ground black pepper

- 1 tablespoon vegetable oil
- 2 tablespoons butter, divided
- 2 medium (2-1/2" dia)s onions, sliced
- 2 medium (2-1/4" to 3" dia, raw)s russet potatoes, peeled and cut into 1-inch cubes
- 2 cloves garlic, crushed
- 1 cup hard apple cider
- 2 tablespoons Dijon mustard
- 1 ½ teaspoons maple syrup
- ¼ teaspoon ground nutmeg
- ¼ cup hot milk

Directions
Step 1
Combine pork chops, salt, thyme, rosemary, and pepper in a resealable plastic bag. Seal and shake until pork chops are coated with seasoning.
Step 2
Turn on a multi-functional pressure cooker (such as Fagor) and select Brown function. Pour in oil. Add pork, with seasoning, and cook until browned, about 5 minutes per side. Transfer to a plate.
Step 3
Melt 1 tablespoon butter in the pot. Cook onions until soft and browned, 8 to 10 minutes. Add potatoes and garlic. Balance pork chops over potatoes.
Step 4
Whisk apple cider, Dijon mustard, maple syrup, and nutmeg in a bowl. Pour over pork chops. Close and lock the lid. Select high pressure according to manufacturer's instructions; set timer for 8 minutes. Allow 10 to 15 minutes for pressure to build.
Step 5
Let pressure release naturally for 5 minutes. Nudge valve slightly open to release remaining pressure more rapidly. Transfer pork chops to a plate.
Step 6
Transfer potatoes and onions to a bowl using a slotted spoon, leaving gravy in the pot. Add remaining 1 tablespoon butter and milk to the potatoes; mash until smooth.
Step 7
Divide mashed potatoes between serving plates. Top with 1 pork chop. Spoon gravy on top.
Cook's Notes:
I don't like underdone meat, so 8 minutes worked well for me. Try 7 minutes if you don't mind some pink in the center.
I found the gravy at the bottom of the pot thick enough without having to simmer it. Set on Simmer for 5 minutes if you want a thicker gravy.
Nutrition Facts
Per Serving:
720.1 calories; protein 38.6g 77% DV; carbohydrates 64.9g 21% DV; fat 29.8g 46% DV; cholesterol 114.2mg 38% DV; sodium 1447.9mg 58% DV.

Brown Rice Buddha Bowl

prep: 30 mins cook: 18 mins total: 48 mins
Servings: 3
Ingredients
- Rice:
- 3 cups water

- 1 cup long-grain brown rice
- ½ teaspoon salt
- Dressing:
- 1 lime, juiced
- 2 tablespoons olive oil
- 1 tablespoon sesame oil
- 1 tablespoon dried Thai basil
- 1 teaspoon minced hot chile pepper
- Vegetables:
- 2 tablespoons sesame seeds
- ½ (8 ounce) package snow peas
- 1 cup cooked chickpeas, drained
- ½ (16 ounce) package firm tofu, cut into strips
- 16 ears baby corn, cut into bite-sized pieces
- 1 cup grated carrots
- 1 small green bell pepper, diced
- 2 eaches green onions, cut on the diagonal
- 2 tablespoons chopped fresh cilantro

Directions
Step 1
Combine water, brown rice, and salt in a pressure cooker. Close and secure the lid; bring to high pressure according to manufacturer's instructions. Cook for 10 minutes. Release pressure naturally according to manufacturer's instructions. Drain any remaining water and transfer rice to a large bowl.
Step 2
Whisk lime juice, olive oil, sesame oil, Thai basil, and chile pepper in a small bowl to make dressing.
Step 3
Toast sesame seeds in a nonstick skillet over medium-low heat, stirring occasionally, until evenly browned and fragrant, about 5 minutes. Transfer to a bowl.
Step 4
Cook and stir snow peas in the same skillet until bright green, 3 to 5 minutes. Remove from heat and let cool.
Step 5
Arrange snow peas, chickpeas, tofu, baby corn, carrots, and green bell pepper over the brown rice. Drizzle dressing over the entire bowl; toss to mix. Sprinkle toasted sesame seeds on top. Garnish with green onions and cilantro.
Cook's Note:
I prefer cooking rice in a pressure cooker. If you want, use your preferred method instead.
Nutrition Facts
Per Serving:
583 calories; protein 18g 36% DV; carbohydrates 80.5g 26% DV; fat 22.6g 35% DV; cholesterolmg; sodium 691.7mg 28% DV.

Instant Pot Mongolian Beef

prep: 10 mins cook: 45 mins additional: 5 mins total: 1 hr
Servings: 8
Ingredients
- 1 head garlic
- 2 pounds flank steak
- 1 pinch salt and ground black pepper to taste
- 1 tablespoon olive oil

- 2 eaches sweet onions (such as Vidalia), cut into wedges
- ⅔ cup dark brown sugar
- ½ cup water
- 1 green bell pepper, sliced
- 1 red bell pepper, sliced
- ½ cup liquid amino acid (such as Bragg)
- ½ teaspoon minced fresh ginger root
- 3 tablespoons water
- 2 tablespoons arrowroot powder
- 3 eaches green onions, cut in 1-inch pieces

Directions
Step 1
Preheat the oven to 350 degrees F (175 degrees C).
Step 2
Brush unpeeled garlic cloves with a small amount of olive oil and wrap in a piece of aluminum foil.
Step 3
Bake in the preheated oven until garlic cloves are tender and browned, about 20 minutes. Let cool; remove skin from cloves.
Step 4
Season steak with salt and pepper. Add oil to a multi-functional pressure cooker (such as Instant Pot) and select Saute function. Cook steak in batches until browned, about 8 minutes. Do not crowd the pot. Transfer beef to a plate.
Step 5
Saute garlic in the pot until fragrant, about 1 minute. Add onions, brown sugar, 1/2 cup water, green bell pepper, red bell pepper, liquid aminos, and ginger. Stir to combine. Add browned beef and any accumulated juices.
Step 6
Close and lock the lid. Select high pressure according to manufacturer's instructions; set timer for 12 minutes. Allow 10 to 15 minutes for pressure to build.
Step 7
Release pressure carefully using the quick-release method according to manufacturer's instructions, about 5 minutes. Unlock and remove the lid.
Step 8
Combine 3 tablespoons water and arrowroot powder in a bowl; whisk until smooth. Add mixture to the sauce in the pot, stirring constantly. Select Simmer mode and bring to a boil; stir constantly until sauce thickens, about 5 minutes. Stir in green onions.
Nutrition Facts
Per Serving:
257.1 calories; protein 16.4g 33% DV; carbohydrates 28.2g 9% DV; fat 10g 15% DV; cholesterol 35.7mg 12% DV; sodium 724.6mg 29% DV.

Instant Pot Beef Pho

prep: 20 mins cook: 53 mins additional: 35 mins total: 1 hr 48 mins
Servings: 6
Ingredients
- 3 pounds beef soup bones
- 3 eaches whole cloves
- 3 eaches whole star anise pods
- 1 (1/2 inch) piece cinnamon stick
- 1 teaspoon olive oil

- 1 large onion, chopped
- 1 (2 inch) piece ginger, peeled
- ½ pound chuck roast
- 2 tablespoons fish sauce
- 1 tablespoon raw sugar
- 2 teaspoons kosher salt
- 9 cups water
- ½ pound top round beef
- 12 ounces dry rice stick noodles
- ¼ cup chopped cilantro
- 2 medium (4-1/8" long)s green onions, chopped

Directions

Step 1
Set an electric pressure cooker (such as Instant Pot) on "Saute" mode. Add beef bones with water to cover; bring to a boil. Boil vigorously for 3 minutes; drain. Transfer bones to a plate. Dry out the pot and return it to the pressure cooker.

Step 2
Set cooker on "Saute" mode. Add cloves, star anise, and cinnamon stick to the bottom of the pot. Toast, turning once to avoid burning, until aromatic, about 5 minutes. Transfer to a bowl.

Step 3
Pour olive oil into the hot pot. Add chopped onion and ginger; cook and stir until softened and starting to brown, about 10 minutes.

Step 4
Place the beef bones, toasted spices, chuck roast, fish sauce, sugar, and salt in the pot. Pour in 9 cups of water, filling the pot 3/4 full. Seal pressure cooker and bring to high pressure according to manufacturer's instructions; cook for 30 minutes. Release pressure through natural-release method for 20 minutes.

Step 5
Remove the chuck roast from the pot. Pour the stock through a sieve into another pot. Discard the bones and spices. Put the pot on the stove, cover, and keep hot over low heat.

Step 6
Place top round into the freezer for 15 minutes. Place rice noodles in a bowl with warm water to cover; soak until pliable, about 15 minutes. Drain the noodles.

Step 7
Remove the top round from the freezer and slice it as thinly as possible, cutting against the grain for best results. Slice the chuck roast.

Step 8
Put a small pile of rice noodles in the middle of a soup bowl. Top with cilantro and green onions. Arrange slices of raw top round and chuck roast around the noodles. Pour in the hot stock, carefully, until the bowl is full. Repeat for additional servings.

Editor's Note:
Consuming raw beef may increase your risk of foodborne illness, especially if you have certain medical conditions.
Nutrition data for this recipe includes the full amount of beef bones and aromatics. The actual amount consumed will vary.

Nutrition Facts
Per Serving:
366.8 calories; protein 17.5g 35% DV; carbohydrates 52.1g 17% DV; fat 8.7g 14% DV; cholesterol 40.2mg 13% DV; sodium 1050.1mg 42% DV

Instant Pot Jamaican Chicken Curry

prep: 15 mins cook: 20 mins additional: 15 mins total: 50 mins
Servings: 6

Ingredients

- 2 tablespoons ghee
- 1 medium onion, chopped
- 1 tablespoon minced garlic
- 1 tablespoon minced fresh ginger
- 2 tablespoons Jamaican curry powder
- 1 fresh jalapeno pepper, seeded and sliced
- ¼ teaspoon ground thyme

- 1 pinch salt and ground black pepper to taste
- 2 cups chicken broth
- 1 ½ pounds boneless, skinless chicken thighs, cut into 3 pieces each
- 2 medium potatoes, peeled and cubed
- 1 pound baby carrots
- 3 cups steamed basmati rice

Directions
Step 1
Turn on a multi-functional pressure cooker (such as Instant Pot) and select Saute function. Heat ghee. Add onion and cook until starting to turn clear, 2 to 3 minutes. Add garlic and ginger and cook, stirring, until garlic is fragrant, about 1 minute. Stir in Jamaican curry powder, jalapeno, thyme, salt, and pepper until well combined.
Step 2
Pour in 1/4 cup of chicken broth, scraping off the browned bits from the bottom of the inner pot. Add chicken pieces, potatoes, and carrots; stir until well coated with the spices and seasonings. Pour in remaining chicken broth. Close and lock the lid.
Step 3
Select high pressure according to manufacturer's instructions; set timer for 6 minutes. Allow 10 to 15 minutes for pressure to build.
Step 4
Release pressure using the natural-release method according to manufacturer's instructions for 10 minutes. Release pressure carefully using the quick-release method, about 5 minutes. Unlock and remove the lid. Serve over steamed rice.
Cook's Note:
Curry from the island adds heat in the pepper selected for the dish. We like mild-flavored curry, so I used a sliced, seeded jalapeno. If you have a more adventurous palate, choose a serrano pepper or even a Scotch Bonnet, for the truly brave!
Nutrition Facts
Per Serving:
329.8 calories; protein 22g 44% DV; carbohydrates 22.7g 7% DV; fat 16.7g 26% DV; cholesterol 83.6mg 28% DV; sodium 542.4mg 22% DV.

Instant Pot Caldillo

prep: 15 mins cook: 1 hr 5 mins additional: 10 mins total: 1 hr 30 mins
Servings: 8
Ingredients
- 2 tablespoons olive oil
- 2 pounds cubed beef stew meat
- 1 onion, diced
- 4 cups beef broth
- 4 eaches russet potatoes, peeled and diced
- 1 (14.5 ounce) can fire-roasted diced tomatoes
- 1 (8 ounce) can chopped green chiles, drained (such as Hatch)
- 2 teaspoons Mexican oregano
- 2 teaspoons minced garlic
- 2 teaspoons cumin
- 1 teaspoon dried chipotle chile powder
- 1 teaspoon chili powder
- ½ teaspoon ground black pepper

Directions
Step 1
Turn on a multi-functional pressure cooker (such as Instant Pot) and select Saute function. Heat olive oil and sear beef cubes until browned on all sides, 5 to 8 minutes. Remove browned beef from the pot and set aside. Add onion and cook until soft and translucent, about 5 minutes. Turn off Saute function.
Step 2
Return beef to the pot with onions. Mix in beef broth, potatoes, diced tomatoes, green chiles, oregano, garlic, cumin, chipotle chile powder, chili powder, and pepper. Close and lock the lid. Select high pressure according to manufacturer's instructions; set timer for 45 minutes. Allow 10 to 15 minutes for pressure to build.
Step 3
Release pressure using the natural-release method according to manufacturer's instructions, 10 to 40 minutes.
Nutrition Facts
Per Serving:
370 calories; protein 23.1g 46% DV; carbohydrates 25.4g 8% DV; fat 19.3g 30% DV; cholesterol 62.6mg 21% DV; sodium 919.6mg 37% DV.

Instant Pot Chicken and Farro Soup

prep: 15 mins cook: 30 mins additional: 15 mins total: 1 hr
Servings: 6

Ingredients
- 2 tablespoons avocado oil
- 2 cups carrots that have been sliced lengthwise and cut into 3/4-inch slices
- 1 cup sliced celery with leaves
- 1 leek, halved lengthwise and sliced
- 1 ½ teaspoons minced garlic
- 2 tablespoons tomato paste
- 1 teaspoon ground thyme
- 1 teaspoon dried oregano
- 1 teaspoon dried parsley
- 1 teaspoon salt
- ½ teaspoon ground black pepper
- 5 cups low-sodium chicken broth
- 1 cup farro, rinsed

- 1 pound skinless, boneless chicken breasts, trimmed

Directions
Step 1
Turn on a multi-functional pressure cooker (such as Instant Pot) and select Saute function. Heat oil in the hot pot and add carrots, celery, and leek. Cook, stirring frequently, until vegetables start to soften, 3 to 4 minutes. Add garlic and cook until just fragrant, about 30 seconds. Add tomato paste and cook for 1 minute. Stir in thyme, oregano, parsley, salt, and pepper. Pour broth into the pot, add farro, and stir. Push chicken breasts down into the liquid. Close and lock the lid.
Step 2
Select high pressure according to manufacturer's instructions; set timer for 12 minutes. Allow 10 to 15 minutes for pressure to build.
Step 3
Release pressure using the natural-release method according to manufacturer's instructions for 10 minutes. Release remaining pressure carefully using the quick-release method according to manufacturer's instructions, about 5 minutes. Unlock and remove the lid. Transfer chicken to a clean work surface and roughly chop; return to the pot and stir. Taste and adjust salt. Serve.
Nutrition Facts
Per Serving:
279.2 calories; protein 22.9g 46% DV; carbohydrates 32g 10% DV; fat 7.9g 12% DV; cholesterol 46.4mg 16% DV; sodium 613.6mg 25% DV.

Instant Pot Chicken Breast (from Fresh or Frozen)

prep: 5 mins cook: 20 mins additional: 10 mins total: 35 mins
Servings: 2
Ingredients

- 1 cup chicken broth
- 1 (16 ounce) skinless, boneless chicken breast
- 1 pinch salt and ground black pepper to taste
- ½ teaspoon paprika
- ½ teaspoon parsley flakes
- ¼ teaspoon dried thyme
- ¼ teaspoon garlic powder

Directions
Step 1
Pour chicken broth into a multi-functional pressure cooker (such as Instant Pot). Add chicken breast and season with salt and pepper.
Step 2
Mix together paprika, parsley, thyme, and garlic powder in a small bowl; sprinkle over chicken. Close and lock the lid. Select high pressure according to manufacturer's instructions; set timer for 10 minutes. Allow 10 minutes for pressure to build.
Step 3

Release pressure using the natural-release method according to manufacturer's instructions, about 10 minutes. Transfer chicken to a cutting board to cool. Chop or shred for later use.

Cook's Note:
You can also use this recipe to cook frozen chicken breasts. If using frozen breasts, run them under water to separate them so that they cook evenly. You'll need to add 6 minutes to the cook time and it will take 15 minutes to come to pressure instead of 10.

Nutrition Facts
Per Serving:
263.2 calories; protein 47.8g 96% DV; carbohydrates 1.4g 1% DV; fat 5.8g 9% DV; cholesterol 131.8mg 44% DV; sodium 773.2mg 31% DV.

Instant Pot Jamaican Chicken Curry

prep: 15 mins cook: 20 mins additional: 15 mins total: 50 mins
Servings: 6

Ingredients

- 2 tablespoons ghee
- 1 medium onion, chopped
- 1 tablespoon minced garlic
- 1 tablespoon minced fresh ginger
- 2 tablespoons Jamaican curry powder
- 1 fresh jalapeno pepper, seeded and sliced
- ¼ teaspoon ground thyme
- 1 pinch salt and ground black pepper to taste
- 2 cups chicken broth
- 1 ½ pounds boneless, skinless chicken thighs, cut into 3 pieces each
- 2 medium potatoes, peeled and cubed
- 1 pound baby carrots
- 3 cups steamed basmati rice

Directions
Step 1
Turn on a multi-functional pressure cooker (such as Instant Pot) and select Saute function. Heat ghee. Add onion and cook until starting to turn clear, 2 to 3 minutes. Add garlic and ginger and cook, stirring, until garlic is fragrant, about 1 minute. Stir in Jamaican curry powder, jalapeno, thyme, salt, and pepper until well combined.

Step 2
Pour in 1/4 cup of chicken broth, scraping off the browned bits from the bottom of the inner pot. Add chicken pieces, potatoes, and carrots; stir until well coated with the spices and seasonings. Pour in remaining chicken broth. Close and lock the lid.

Step 3
Select high pressure according to manufacturer's instructions; set timer for 6 minutes. Allow 10 to 15 minutes for pressure to build.

Step 4
Release pressure using the natural-release method according to manufacturer's instructions for 10 minutes. Release pressure carefully using the quick-release method, about 5 minutes. Unlock and remove the lid. Serve over steamed rice.

Cook's Note:

Curry from the island adds heat in the pepper selected for the dish. We like mild-flavored curry, so I used a sliced, seeded jalapeno. If you have a more adventurous palate, choose a serrano pepper or even a Scotch Bonnet, for the truly brave!
Nutrition Facts
Per Serving:
329.8 calories; protein 22g 44% DV; carbohydrates 22.7g 7% DV; fat 16.7g 26% DV; cholesterol 83.6mg 28% DV; sodium 542.4mg 22% DV.

Pressure Cooker Italian Chicken Soup

prep: 25 mins cook: 25 mins total: 50 mins
Servings: 8
Ingredients

- 2 teaspoons olive oil
- 4 eaches Italian turkey sausage links, casings removed
- 1 medium onion, diced
- 3 cloves garlic, minced
- ½ cup pearl barley
- 1 cup green lentils
- 1 bone-in chicken breast half, skin removed
- ½ cup chopped fresh parsley
- 3 cups chicken stock
- 1 (15 ounce) can chickpeas (garbanzo beans), drained
- 1 (16 ounce) bag fresh spinach leaves, chopped
- 1 cup mild salsa

Directions
Step 1
heat 1 teaspoon olive oil in a pressure cooker over medium heat. Add sausage meat, and cook until browned, breaking it into crumbles. Remove sausage to a plate and drain oil. Add another 1 teaspoon of olive oil to pressure cooker; cook onion and garlic until onion is transparent. Add barley and stir 1 minute. Return sausage to pressure cooker. Add lentils, chicken, parsley, and chicken stock to cooker, adding enough stock to completely cover chicken. Close cover securely; place pressure regulator on vent pipe. Bring pressure cooker to full pressure over high heat (this may take 15 minutes). Reduce heat to medium high; cook for 9 minutes. Pressure regulator should maintain a slow steady rocking motion; adjust heat if necessary.
Step 2
Remove pressure cooker from heat; use quick-release following manufacturer's instructions or allow pressure to drop on its own. Open cooker and remove chicken; shred meat and return to soup. Add garbanzo beans, spinach and salsa; stir to blend and heat through before serving.
Nutrition Facts
Per Serving:
244.7 calories; protein 17.4g 35% DV; carbohydrates 37.3g 12% DV; fat 3.3g 5% DV; cholesterol 16.2mg 5% DV; sodium 527.1mg 21% DV.

Instant Pot Orange Chicken

prep: 15 mins cook: 35 mins additional: 20 mins total: 1 hr 10 mins
Servings: 8
Ingredients

- 3 pounds skinless, boneless chicken
- 2 tablespoons oil
- ¾ cup orange juice
- 1 (8 ounce) can tomato sauce
- ¼ cup white sugar
- ¼ cup blackstrap molasses
- ¼ cup soy sauce
- 4 cloves garlic, minced
- 1 orange, zested and juiced, divided
- 1 tablespoon grated fresh ginger
- 1 tablespoon rice wine
- 3 tablespoons cornstarch

Directions
Step 1
Blot chicken with paper towels until completely dry. Cut into 1- to 2-inch chunks.
Step 2
Turn on a multi-functional pressure cooker (such as Instant Pot), select Saute function, and click to adjust to the highest heat. When the pot is hot, add oil and heat until shimmering. Add chicken and saute until it starts to get golden, stirring constantly so it doesn't stick to the bottom of the pot, for 2 to 3 minutes. Pour 3/4 cup orange juice into the pot and bring to a boil while scraping all the browned bits of food off the bottom of the pan with a wooden spoon.
Step 3
Add tomato sauce, sugar, molasses, soy sauce, garlic, orange zest, ginger, and rice wine; gently stir until all ingredients are combined and coated in sauce. Cancel Saute function.
Step 4
Close and lock the lid, and make sure the vent is closed. Select high pressure according to manufacturer's instructions; set timer for 5 minutes. Allow 10 to 15 minutes for pressure to build.
Step 5
Allow the Instant Pot to remain on for 10 minutes with the Keep Warm function. Release pressure carefully using the quick-release method according to manufacturer's instructions, about 5 minutes. Unlock and remove the lid. Select Saute function and click to adjust to the lowest heat.
Step 6
Combine 3 tablespoons freshly squeezed orange juice with cornstarch in a medium bowl; whisk until combined with no lumps. Add to the Instant Pot and stir to combine. Cook, stirring gently, until sauce thickens, about 3 minutes. Simmer for 2 to 3 minutes more.
Step 7
Cancel Saute function and let stand until sauce thickens further, 5 to 7 minutes. Serve.
Nutrition Facts
Per Serving:
296.2 calories; protein 34.3g 69% DV; carbohydrates 22.3g 7% DV; fat 7g 11% DV; cholesterol 87.9mg 29% DV; sodium 674.3mg 27% DV.

Unsweetened Fig Butter

prep: 10 mins cook: 15 mins additional: 5 mins total: 30 mins
Servings: 8
Ingredients
- 15 figs dried figs
- 2 eaches large pitted dates
- 2 cups water to cover

Directions
Step 1
Place figs and dates into a multi-functional pressure cooker (such as Instant Pot). Add enough water to cover. Close and lock the lid and seal the vent. Select high pressure according to manufacturer's instructions; set timer for 3 minutes. Allow 10 to 15 minutes for pressure to build.
Step 2
Release pressure carefully using the quick-release method according to manufacturer's instructions, about 5 minutes. Unlock and remove the lid.
Step 3
Spoon figs and dates from the pot, pressing gently on them using another spoon to drain their liquid back into the pot. Place figs and dates into a food processor. Pulse until smooth, scraping down the bowl as needed.
Step 4
Transfer fig butter to an airtight container and store in the refrigerator.
Cook's Notes:
Use for toast, biscuits, a sandwich spread, or on a meat and cheese platter.
This fig butter freezes very well, so feel free to double or triple the recipe.
Nutrition Facts
Per Serving:
110.8 calories; protein 1.3g 3% DV; carbohydrates 28.6g 9% DV; fat 0.4g 1% DV; cholesterolmg; sodium 5.8mg.

Instant Pot Colorado Chile Verde

prep: 15 mins cook: 50 mins additional: 15 mins total: 1 hr 20 mins
Servings: 8
Ingredients

- 1 tablespoon olive oil
- 1 pound chicken breasts, cubed, or more to taste
- ½ large onion, diced
- 2 eaches roasted Hatch chile peppers - seeded, de-veined, and diced, or more to taste
- 3 cloves garlic, minced
- 1 tablespoon ground cumin
- ½ teaspoon salt
- ½ teaspoon freshly ground black pepper
- 2 cups chicken broth
- 1 (16 ounce) jar salsa verde (green salsa)
- 1 (15.5 ounce) can white beans, drained and rinsed
- 2 ears corn, kernels cut from cob
- ¼ cup minced cilantro
- ¼ cup all-purpose flour
- 1 tablespoon potato starch

- 2 tablespoons cold water
- 1 lime, cut into wedges

Directions
Step 1
Turn on a multi-functional pressure cooker (such as Instant Pot), select Saute function, and add olive oil. Add chicken breast, onion, chile peppers, garlic, cumin, salt, and pepper to hot oil. Saute until chicken is browned and onions are soft and translucent, about 5 minutes. Add chicken broth, salsa verde, white beans, corn kernels, and cilantro; mix well. Turn off Saute mode.
Step 2
Close and lock the lid. Select high pressure according to manufacturer's instructions; set timer for 30 minutes. Allow 10 to 15 minutes for pressure to build.
Step 3
Release pressure using the natural-release method according to manufacturer's instructions, about 15 minutes. Unlock and remove the lid. Select Saute function. Stir in flour and cook chile until it thickens, 1 to 2 minutes. If you like a thicker consistency, mix potato starch and water in a small bowl and stir into chile with the flour. Serve with lime wedges.
Nutrition Facts
Per Serving:
337.2 calories; protein 26.8g 54% DV; carbohydrates 48.6g 16% DV; fat 4.2g 6% DV; cholesterol 33.8mg 11% DV; sodium 666.4mg 27% DV.

Saffron Risotto in the Pressure Cooker

prep: 5 mins cook: 10 mins additional: 10 mins total: 25 mins
Servings: 4
Ingredients
- 1 pinch saffron
- ⅓ cup hot water
- 4 tablespoons butter, divided
- 1 small shallot, finely chopped
- 1 ½ cups Arborio rice
- ¾ cup dry white wine
- 3 ¼ cups boiling vegetable stock
- ⅓ cup grated Parmesan cheese
- 1 pinch salt and freshly ground black pepper to taste
- ¼ cup grated Parmesan cheese, or to taste

Directions
Step 1
Soak saffron threads in hot water in a bowl.
Step 2
Melt 2 1/2 tablespoons butter in a pressure cooker over low heat. Cook and stir shallot until soft, about 3 minutes. Add rice; cook and stir for a few minutes until rice has absorbed butter and is toasted, about 3 minutes. Pour in wine and allow alcohol to cook off, about 1 minute. Add boiling stock all at once and stir. Close cooker securely and place pressure regulator over vent according to manufacturer's instructions. Increase heat to high. Heat until steam escapes in a steady flow and makes a whistling sound. Reduce heat to low and cook for 4 minutes.
Step 3
Remove cooker from heat and release pressure carefully using the quick-release method according to manufacturer's instructions, about 5 minutes. Carefully open

once pressure is completely released and stir well. Stir in saffron, remaining 1 1/2 tablespoon butter, Parmesan cheese, salt, and pepper.
Step 4
Let risotto rest for 3 minutes in order to expand, soak up the stock, and absorb flavor. Serve in warmed bowls with extra grated Parmesan cheese.
Cook's Notes:
You can cook any kind of risotto in a pressure cooker. Simply cook the other ingredients (such as mushrooms, pancetta, or seafood) separately and add to the rice at the end. If using ingredients that require a longer cooking time (like fresh artichokes) you can start by cooking them in the pressure cooker, then adding the rice and finishing all together. If you have an Instant Pot(R) you can prepare the ingredients in the Instant Pot(R) on Saute mode.
There are 3 rules when cooking risotto in pressure cooker. First, the amount of stock has to be slightly more than two times the rice, about 20% more than double. For a creamier risotto, use more stock. Second, the cooking time is 4 minutes sharp after the first whistling. Not one minute longer, not one minute less. When you open the cooker, the rice will feel still uncooked but it will get soft in the 3 minutes of resting. Third, do not skip the resting time. It is essential for the rice to relax, release starch, and get that creamy texture typical of risotto.
Nutrition Facts
Per Serving:
523.3 calories; protein 11.3g 23% DV; carbohydrates 75.2g 24% DV; fat 15.3g 24% DV; cholesterol 40.8mg 14% DV; sodium 676.6mg 27% DV.

Instant Pot Chilorio

prep: 25 mins cook: 30 mins additional: 25 mins total: 1 hr 20 mins
Servings: 10

Ingredients

- 2 ½ pounds pork shoulder, trimmed and cut into 1-inch cubes
- 4 eaches oranges, juiced
- 1 (14.25 ounce) can low-sodium chicken broth
- 1 onion, sliced and separated into rings
- 1 teaspoon dried oregano
- 3 peppers dried ancho chiles (poblanos), stemmed and torn into small pieces
- 2 cups boiling water
- ¼ cup apple cider vinegar
- 1 jalapeno, seeded and chopped
- 2 garlic clove (blank)s garlic cloves
- 2 tablespoons chopped cilantro
- ¼ teaspoon ground cumin

Directions
Step 1
Combine pork, orange juice, broth, onion, and oregano in the inner pot of an electric pressure cooker (such as Instant Pot). Close and lock the lid. Select high pressure according to manufacturer's instructions; set timer for 20 minutes. Allow 10 to 15 minutes for pressure to build.
Step 2

Release pressure using the natural-release method according to manufacturer's instructions, 10 to 40 minutes. Unlock and remove lid.
Step 3
Remove pork from the pot and drain. Transfer to a serving dish.
Step 4
Place ancho chiles in a heat-proof bowl. Pour boiling water over chiles and soak for 15 minutes. Drain chiles, reserving soaking water.
Step 5
Combine 1/2 cup chile soaking water, soaked ancho chiles, apple cider vinegar, jalapeno pepper, garlic, cilantro, and cumin in a blender. Blend to form a thick sauce. Pour sauce over pork and mix well.
You can get a second wind out of your Instant Pot Chilorio with these Torta Sandwiches by user Betty Soup:
Stir together 1 thinly sliced red onion, 3 tablespoons cider vinegar, and 1 teaspoon sugar in a small bowl. Let stand at least 1 hour. Drain. Reheat 1 1/3 cups pork and sauce, covered, in a 2-quart saucepan over medium heat, 5 to 7 minutes. Mash 1 avocado and spread over the bottom half of 4 toasted buns. Top each bun with 1/3 cup pork and sauce and red onion mixture.
Nutrition Facts
Per Serving:
309.1 calories; protein 16.6g 33% DV; carbohydrates 14.9g 5% DV; fat 20.7g 32% DV; cholesterol 65.5mg 22% DV; sodium 1339.7mg 54% DV.

Instant Pot Fresh Steamed Oysters with Spicy Butter

prep: 5 mins cook: 20 mins additional: 5 mins total: 30 mins
Servings: 20

Ingredients

- 1 cup water
- 20 eaches fresh oysters in shells, rinsed and scrubbed clean
- 2 teaspoons Mexican-style hot sauce (such as Valentina)
- ½ teaspoon dried parsley flakes
- 4 tablespoons unsalted butter, melted

Directions
Step 1
Pour water into a multi-functional pressure cooker (such as Instant Pot) and set trivet inside. Place oysters on the trivet. Close and lock the lid. Select Steam function according to manufacturer's instructions; set timer for 2 minutes. Allow 15 minutes for pressure to build.
Step 2
Meanwhile, stir hot sauce and parsley into the melted butter until well combined.
Step 3
Release pressure using quick release according to manufacture's directions, 3 to 5 minutes.
Step 4

Carefully open the oysters using a spoon; set on a serving plate. Spoon butter over the top.
Nutrition Facts
Per Serving:
97.4 calories; protein 3.5g 7% DV; carbohydrates 4.6g 2% DV; fat 7.2g 11% DV; cholesterol 37.7mg 13% DV; sodium 175.9mg 7% DV.

Instant Pot Cream of Asparagus Soup

prep: 10 mins cook: 15 mins additional: 20 mins total: 45 mins
Servings: 4
Ingredients
- 1 tablespoon olive oil
- 4 slices bacon, diced
- ½ onion, diced
- 3 cloves garlic, minced
- 2 pounds asparagus, cut into 1 1/2-inch pieces
- 2 ½ cups chicken broth
- 1 teaspoon salt
- ½ teaspoon ground black pepper
- 1 cup heavy whipping cream

Directions
Step 1
Turn on a multi-functional pressure cooker (such as Instant Pot), select Saute function, and add olive oil. Add bacon to warmed oil and saute for 2 minutes. Stir in onion and continue cooking until onion is soft and translucent, about 5 minutes. Add garlic and asparagus. Cook 1 to 2 minutes.
Step 2
Pour chicken broth over asparagus mixture and bring to a boil. Turn Saute mode off and press the Manual mode. Close and lock the lid. Select High pressure according to manufacturer's instructions; set timer for 5 minutes. Allow 10 to 15 minutes for pressure to build.
Step 3
Release pressure using the natural-release method according to manufacturer's instructions, 10 to 40 minutes. Unlock and remove the lid.
Step 4
Puree asparagus mixture with an immersion blender until smooth. Mix in cream and select Saute function. Cook until soup is warmed through, but not boiling. Taste and season with salt and pepper.
Nutrition Facts
Per Serving:
355.9 calories; protein 10.8g 22% DV; carbohydrates 14.9g 5% DV; fat 29.8g 46% DV; cholesterol 95.2mg 32% DV; sodium 1545.4mg 62% DV.

Potato Soup or Chowder

prep: 20 mins cook: 20 mins additional: 5 mins total: 45 mins
Servings: 6
Ingredients

- 6 eaches potatoes, cut into cubes, or more as needed
- 2 ½ cups chicken stock
- 1 cup diced onion
- 1 cup chopped carrots
- 1 cup chopped celery
- 2 tablespoons all-purpose flour
- 2 teaspoons salt
- 1 teaspoon ground black pepper
- 1 (15.25 ounce) can whole kernel corn, drained
- 1 cup cooked turkey ham, cut into 1/4-inch cubes
- 2 cups shredded Cheddar cheese

Directions
Step 1
Combine potatoes, chicken stock, onion, carrots, celery, flour, salt, and pepper in a multi-functional pressure cooker (such as Instant Pot). Close and lock the lid. Select high pressure according to manufacturer's instructions; set timer for 10 minutes. Allow 10 to 15 minutes for pressure to build.
Step 2
Release pressure carefully using the quick-release method according to manufacturer's instructions, about 5 minutes. Unlock and remove lid. Stir in corn and turkey ham. Add Cheddar cheese; stir until melted.
Cook's Notes:
Dice potatoes into smaller pieces for a creamier soup.
Bouillon, chicken soup base, or milk may be substituted for the chicken stock. Processed cheese food (such as Velveeta(R)) or any of your preferred cheese can be substituted for the Cheddar cheese.
You can use 1 packet country gravy mix in place of the flour.
If potatoes are not done to your liking, cook on High/Soup setting (not pressure)for a few minutes more.
Nutrition Facts
Per Serving:
450.5 calories; protein 23.6g 47% DV; carbohydrates 58.9g 19% DV; fat 14.9g 23% DV; cholesterol 57.6mg 19% DV; sodium 1567.9mg 63% DV.

Instant Pot Cream of Asparagus Soup

prep: 10 mins cook: 15 mins additional: 20 mins total: 45 mins
Servings: 4
Ingredients

- 1 tablespoon olive oil
- 4 slices bacon, diced
- ½ onion, diced
- 3 cloves garlic, minced
- 2 pounds asparagus, cut into 1 1/2-inch pieces
- 2 ½ cups chicken broth
- 1 teaspoon salt
- ½ teaspoon ground black pepper
- 1 cup heavy whipping cream

Directions
Step 1
Turn on a multi-functional pressure cooker (such as Instant Pot), select Saute function, and add olive oil. Add bacon to warmed oil and saute for 2 minutes. Stir in onion and continue cooking until onion is soft and translucent, about 5 minutes. Add garlic and asparagus. Cook 1 to 2 minutes.
Step 2
Pour chicken broth over asparagus mixture and bring to a boil. Turn Saute mode off and press the Manual mode. Close and lock the lid. Select High pressure according to manufacturer's instructions; set timer for 5 minutes. Allow 10 to 15 minutes for pressure to build.
Step 3
Release pressure using the natural-release method according to manufacturer's instructions, 10 to 40 minutes. Unlock and remove the lid.
Step 4
Puree asparagus mixture with an immersion blender until smooth. Mix in cream and select Saute function. Cook until soup is warmed through, but not boiling. Taste and season with salt and pepper.
Nutrition Facts
Per Serving:
355.9 calories; protein 10.8g 22% DV; carbohydrates 14.9g 5% DV; fat 29.8g 46% DV; cholesterol 95.2mg 32% DV; sodium 1545.4mg 62% DV.

Potato Soup or Chowder

prep: 20 mins cook: 20 mins additional: 5 mins total: 45 mins
Servings: 6
Ingredients

- 6 eaches potatoes, cut into cubes, or more as needed
- 2 ½ cups chicken stock
- 1 cup diced onion
- 1 cup chopped carrots
- 1 cup chopped celery
- 2 tablespoons all-purpose flour
- 2 teaspoons salt
- 1 teaspoon ground black pepper
- 1 (15.25 ounce) can whole kernel corn, drained
- 1 cup cooked turkey ham, cut into 1/4-inch cubes
- 2 cups shredded Cheddar cheese

Directions
Step 1
Combine potatoes, chicken stock, onion, carrots, celery, flour, salt, and pepper in a multi-functional pressure cooker (such as Instant Pot). Close and lock the lid. Select high pressure according to manufacturer's instructions; set timer for 10 minutes. Allow 10 to 15 minutes for pressure to build.
Step 2
Release pressure carefully using the quick-release method according to manufacturer's instructions, about 5 minutes. Unlock and remove lid. Stir in corn and turkey ham. Add Cheddar cheese; stir until melted.
Cook's Notes:
Dice potatoes into smaller pieces for a creamier soup.
Bouillon, chicken soup base, or milk may be substituted for the chicken stock.

Processed cheese food (such as Velveeta(R)) or any of your preferred cheese can be substituted for the Cheddar cheese.
You can use 1 packet country gravy mix in place of the flour.
If potatoes are not done to your liking, cook on High/Soup setting (not pressure)for a few minutes more.
Nutrition Facts
Per Serving:
450.5 calories; protein 23.6g 47% DV; carbohydrates 58.9g 19% DV; fat 14.9g 23% DV; cholesterol 57.6mg 19% DV; sodium 1567.9mg 63% DV.

Instant Pot Chicken and Rice Soup

prep: 25 mins cook: 30 mins additional: 10 mins total: 1 hr 5 mins
Servings: 4
Ingredients

- 1 ½ cups low-sodium chicken broth
- ⅓ cup brown rice
- 1 ½ pounds chicken breast tenderloins, cubed
- 1 large onion, diced
- 1 ½ cups diced carrot
- 1 ½ cups diced celery
- 1 cup frozen corn kernels
- 1 teaspoon garlic powder
- 1 teaspoon onion powder
- 1 teaspoon poultry seasoning
- ½ teaspoon dried thyme
- ½ teaspoon salt
- ½ teaspoon ground black pepper
- ½ cup half-and-half
- 2 teaspoons cornstarch
- ½ cup frozen peas

Directions
Step 1
Stir together broth and brown rice in a multi-functional pressure cooker until rice is moistened. Add chicken, onion, carrot, celery, corn, garlic powder, onion powder, poultry seasoning, thyme, salt, and pepper. Close and lock the lid.
Step 2
Select high pressure and set timer for 18 minutes. Allow 10 to 15 minutes for pressure to build.
Step 3
Release pressure naturally, about 10 minutes. Carefully release remaining pressure using the quick-release method. Remove lid.
Step 4
Stir together half-and-half and cornstarch in a small bowl. Add to cooker, along with peas, and stir. Select Saute function; cook, stirring constantly, until thickened and bubbly, 2 to 3 minutes.
Nutrition Facts
Per Serving:
380.2 calories; protein 40g 80% DV; carbohydrates 36.9g 12% DV; fat 8.2g 13% DV; cholesterol 100.5mg 34% DV; sodium 511.7mg 21% DV.

Instant Pot Lebanese Lentil Soup (Shorbat Adas)

prep: 25 mins cook: 25 mins additional: 5 mins total: 55 mins
Servings: 4
Ingredients

- 2 tablespoons extra-virgin olive oil
- 1 onion, finely chopped
- 1 Yukon Gold potato, peeled and diced
- 1 carrot, peeled and diced
- 1 tomato, diced
- 2 rib (blank)s celery ribs, diced
- 1 clove garlic, chopped, or more to taste
- 1 ½ teaspoons kosher salt
- ¾ teaspoon ground cumin
- ⅛ teaspoon ground cinnamon
- ⅛ teaspoon allspice
- 4 cups low-sodium vegetable broth
- 2 cups water
- 1 ½ cups red lentils
- 2 fruit, without seeds lemons
- 2 eaches pita bread, cut into squares
- 1 cooking spray
- 1 pinch salt

Directions
Step 1
Preheat the oven to 400 degrees F (200 degrees C).
Step 2
Turn on a multi-functional pressure cooker (such as Instant Pot) and select Saute function. Heat olive oil in the pot. Add onion, potato, carrot, tomato, celery, and garlic; cook and stir until starting to soften, 3 to 5 minutes. Sprinkle salt, cumin, cinnamon, and allspice over the vegetables and stir until fragrant.
Step 3
Pour in stock, water, and lentils. Close and lock the lid. Select high pressure according to manufacturer's instructions; set timer for 10 minutes. Allow 10 to 15 minutes for pressure to build.
Step 4
Meanwhile, spread pita squares on a lined baking sheet. Spray with cooking spray and season with salt.
Step 5
Bake in the preheated oven until toasted, about 8 minutes.
Step 6
Release pressure carefully using the quick-release method according to manufacturer's instructions, about 5 minutes. Unlock and remove the lid. Puree soup using an immersion blender. Stir in juice of 1 lemon.
Step 7
Divide soup among bowls and scatter a handful of pita chips over each. Cut the second lemon into wedges and serve alongside.
Cook's Note:
This soup tends to thicken as it sits. You can thin leftovers with some water when reheating.
Nutrition Facts
Per Serving:

456.2 calories; protein 23.2g 46% DV; carbohydrates 76.7g 25% DV; fat 8.9g 14% DV; cholesterolmg; sodium 1139.3mg 46% DV.

Instant Pot Cheddar Cheese Sauce

prep: 5 mins cook: 10 mins total: 15 mins
Servings: 6
Ingredients
- ¼ cup butter
- 1 teaspoon salt
- 1 teaspoon ground black pepper
- 1 teaspoon onion powder
- 2 tablespoons tapioca starch
- 1 ¼ cups whole milk
- 1 ½ cups sharp Cheddar cheese, grated

Directions
Step 1
Turn on a multi-functional pressure cooker (such as Instant Pot) and select the Saute function. Add butter and let it melt. Season with salt, pepper, and onion powder and stir. Sprinkle with tapioca starch and stir roux until blended; it will be thick.
Step 2
Pour in milk gradually, 1/4 cup at a time, stirring each addition until well combined. Keep stirring to remove clumps. Sauce should be creamy and just under boiling temperature. If it starts to boil, turn Instant Pot off and set to Keep Warm.
Step 3
Add Cheddar cheese and stir continuously until cheese has melted and is well combined into the sauce.
Nutrition Facts
Per Serving:
223.4 calories; protein 8.8g 18% DV; carbohydrates 5.4g 2% DV; fat 18.7g 29% DV; cholesterol 55.1mg 18% DV; sodium 638.3mg 26% DV.

Instant Pot Egg Bite

sprep: 15 mins cook: 13 mins additional: 10 mins total: 38 mins
Servings: 6
Ingredients

- 12 eaches eggs
- 1 teaspoon granulated garlic
- 1 ½ teaspoons salt, or to taste
- 1 ½ teaspoons ground black pepper, or to taste
- 1 cup chopped spinach
- ¾ cup shredded Muenster cheese
- ½ cup chopped onion

Directions
Step 1
Beat eggs in a medium bowl until yellow and frothy. Add garlic, salt, and pepper.
Step 2

Toss spinach, Muenster cheese, and onion together in a small bowl. Divide evenly among the cavities of a silicone egg mold. Pour beaten eggs into each cavity, filling each 3/4 full. Cover mold with aluminum foil.
Step 3
Pour 1/2 cup water into a multi-functional pressure cooker (such as Instant Pot). Place egg mold inside. Close and lock the lid, sealing the vent. Select Steam function; set timer for 13 minutes.
Step 4
Release pressure naturally according to manufacturer's instructions, 10 to 40 minutes.
Nutrition Facts
Per Serving:
187.1 calories; protein 14.8g 30% DV; carbohydrates 3g 1% DV; fat 13g 20% DV; cholesterol 340.9mg 114% DV; sodium 798.1mg 32% DV.